SUCCESS IS THE ONLY OPTION

ALSO BY JOHN CALIPARI

Players First

Bounce Back

Refuse to Lose

Basketball's Half-Court Defense

SUCCESS IS THE ONLY OPTION

THE ART OF COACHING EXTREME TALENT

JOHN CALIPARI

AND MICHAEL SOKOLOVE

HARPER

An Imprint of HarperCollinsPublishers

HarperCollins books may be purchased for educational, business, or sales promotional use. For information, please email the Special Markets Department at SPsales@harpercollins.com.

FIRST EDITION

Designed by William Ruoto

Basketball hoop and ball (basketball hoop with basketball, basketball and hoop) by: Tetiana Yurchenko/Shutterstock

High contrast silhouette illustration of an athlete slam dunking a basketball by: ARENA Creative/Shutterstock

Library of Congress Cataloging-in-Publication Data has been applied for.

ISBN 978-0-06-244045-7

16 17 18 19 20 RRD 10 9 8 7 6 5 4 3 2 1

To my late mother, Donna, the original pay-it-forward,

dream-big-dreams person in my life; and my father, Vince,

a true grinder and gatherer who showed me how to

work hard and bring people together.

CONTENTS

Introduction: Appeal to Their Aspirations, Not Their Egos   XIII

1 Assembling the Talent   1

Character Comes First   7
A Lively Mind   12
The Relationship Between Passion and "The Grind"   13
Be Willing to Be Surprised (or, How I Fell in Love
     with a Tiny Point Guard)   17
Seek Out Risk-Takers   24
Talent Flocks Together   27

2 Know the Red Flags   31

Avoid Blame-Shifters   33
A Profile in Accountability   37
Anthony Davis on Being Recruited by Coach Calipari   38

3 Unpack Your Bags   41

Creating Joy   43
Settled In? Okay, Now It's Time to Get Uncomfortable   45
Turning Setbacks into Growth   52
Karl-Anthony Towns on Staying in the Present   59
The Past Is the Past   59

4 Keeping It Real   67

The Tone Changes. The Message Does Not   70
John Robic on the Early Years   74
You Have to Cure Them of Their Delusions   75
Keep It Real, but Don't Be Intimidating   80
You Must Give Recognition (and Also Be Ready
    to Take Responsibility)   83
Tailor the Message to the Individual   90
Don't Be Afraid of Pushback   96

5 The Metrics Don't Lie   101

Keep Score Every Day   102
The Best "System" Is the One That Works   107
Use the Numbers to Promote Certain Behaviors   109
Let the Numbers Tell a Story   111

6 You Can't Delegate Love   117

You Are the Caretaker of Their Dreams   122
Leverage Your Own Success as a Tool of Persuasion   126
If You're Given a Competitive Advantage, Milk It   130
Orlando Antigua (Excerpt)   132
Efficiency, Not Volume   133
Finding Different Sources of Inspiration   137
Embracing the Challenge   139

7 Just Do What You Do Best ... Play to
Your Strengths   145

Demonstrated Performance Builds Confidence   150
They Build Their Own Swagger   155
Ask a Different Question   158
They Are Each on Their Own Path   165
Devin Booker on His Kentucky Experience   171

8 Empowering Your Team   175

Be Random Yet Organized   176
Ignore the Barking Dogs   179
Everybody Has a Different Seat on the Bus   181
The Importance of Nonnegotiables   186
What Were You Doing Before the Camera Focused on You?   189

You Don't Have to Make Them All, but You Can't Miss
   Them All   191
Good Players Make Hard Plays Look Easy, Bad Ones Make
   Easy Plays Look Hard   194
Empowered Teams Have Servant Leaders   196

9   Make It About Something Bigger   203

If It's Predictable, It's Preventable   204
Dealing with Social Media   207
Cultivating Curious Minds   210
When It's Time to Let Go   213
Measurable Results in the NBA   218
Being About Other People   220
My Purpose   222

Afterword   225
Acknowledgments   227

APPEAL TO THEIR
ASPIRATIONS,
NOT THEIR EGOS

A s head basketball coach at the University of Kentucky, I
work with a small group of prodigies. They're like other
highly advanced young people who are seemingly headed
straight to the top of their chosen fields. But the young men
I lead happen to be bigger and more famous, and they do their
work—and their growing up—in public.

They arrive on campus at seventeen or eighteen years old with a
mix of confidence, bravado, and anxiety. Their personal highlight
reels—soaring dunks and three-point shots (just the ones that go
in)—have been up on YouTube since they were in middle school.
It's a lot to live up to. I never want to make them feel less confident
about themselves, but I do tell them: What got you here is not

what's going to get you where you want to go. My job is to serve their aspirations, not their egos.

In recent seasons, I've coached players who left our college program and became almost instant NBA stars: John Wall, DeMarcus Cousins, Anthony Davis, and Karl-Anthony Towns. At Memphis, I had Derrick Rose, who was the league's MVP before he turned twenty-three. Many of my other former players have quickly established themselves in professional basketball and are now on the cusp of stardom.

They are what extreme talent in my business looks like: a mix of size, speed, strength, leaping ability, court vision, ball handling, and shooting acumen. You don't need to have all of these attributes, but if you combine several of them, it can put you among the elite. Sometimes just one of these traits, in excess, is enough to build on. Devin Booker, a freshman on my 2014–15 team, comes to mind. He had a reputation as "just a shooter," but he used that as a foundation and then put in the work to add other valuable aspects to his game. He demonstrates a sometimes overlooked element of extreme talent: a mental makeup that allows a person to truly self-assess.

Intelligence also matters, much more than some people believe it does in my business. I've never met a star who could not think quickly on his feet and reason at a high level. There's only so far you can go in basketball, and most other sports, without being a pretty smart person. My best players, without exception, have been among my most intelligent players—not in all cases top-notch students, especially if they came from struggling school systems, but they had minds that were fast and nimble.

Every one of the players whom I would categorize as an extreme talent shared one other trait: a strong inner drive to succeed. I didn't give them that. I can't give someone that. They had it already. But I had to understand the source of their drive and tap into it. Were they motivated by a fear that they weren't good enough? A chip on their shoulders, because someone along the way had discredited their abilities? A desire to financially prosper and help family members and others back home?

All of them knew they were unfinished products. They needed and wanted to get better, and they put their trust in me and our staff to help them.

There's an old adage that one sign of intelligence is the ability to keep two opposing ideas in your head at the same time and still function. The saying is a pretty good description of what I confront in my job and I believe it applies to anyone—coach, CEO, military leader, teacher, even a parent—who is seeking to lead and inspire highly talented individuals. Those under your command, by definition, are going to be more complicated. They're highly gifted but undeveloped. (Their gifts, in fact, may have delayed other aspects of their development.)

Nothing is more important to me than helping my players reach their individual goals. It is the basis of my "players first" philosophy. But at the same time, I am the leader of an enterprise that cannot succeed unless we march forward together. For that to happen, I must persuade these gifted athletes to share, communicate, bond, and sacrifice for one another. I have to make them understand that they will not reach their own goals unless they can demonstrate these qualities.

I don't recruit anyone who I believe is inherently selfish. But my players have been, by and large, solo performers until they landed on campus. They were celebrated and rewarded for their individual brilliance. It's what first got college coaches sending them letters, traveling to gyms to watch them play, and sitting in their living rooms. It may seem paradoxical, but one way I get them to commit to team basketball—selfless basketball—is by making them understand it is in their self-interest to do so.

It's not easy. You are dealing with a kid who has just chosen your program over countless others, all of which are also led by well-known, successful coaches. He may have announced his decision in a press conference inside his packed high school gymnasium, which was covered live by ESPN. Or maybe he skipped that ritual and just put the news out to his tens of thousands of Twitter followers. Either way, he's coming to you straight from a pedestal.

I'm competitive, of course. Every coach is. I want to win every time we take the court but the reality is that almost every season ends with a loss. At that final moment, I've lost not just a game but a team I wanted to keep coaching and kids I'm not ready to let go. It hurts every time and it can feel like a failure—even though I know it's not.

It would be far worse, though, to fail any of the individuals I coach, and that's the one thing that I can't ever let happen. I recruit kids who expect to proceed to the NBA, and for most, it's a reasonable expectation. If I nurture them correctly, some of them can make up to $500 million or more over their professional basketball careers.

Their futures, on some level, may seem promised to them. One thing I'm always cognizant of is that they have the potential to experience crushing disappointment at a younger age than most. They have an opportunity to succeed on a grand scale—or, it may seem to them, to fall far short of expectations.

I have to be patient because I'm asking for things that they have never given before. But I'm working against the clock. It's another of those seeming contradictions. My patience is balanced against the reality that time is always in short supply. My players need my support but I can't slow the train down to coddle them.

Every new season for us is a start-up. We're like a high-tech firm working to put out a highly anticipated new product. People are waiting to see if it's great or if it's a bust. The difference is, we've got no runway. We play a five-month season, and at the end we're judged as a team and as individuals. And then our best performers leave and I have to start all over again with a new group. I did not advocate for the "one and done" era in college basketball, but I have embraced the reality of it. It didn't scare me, and I've made it work for the players and the program.

I'm now in my twenty-fifth season as a college head coach, having spent the last eight seasons at Kentucky. When I look back at where I came from—a tiny house in Moon Township, Pennsylvania, outside Pittsburgh, the son of an airport baggage handler and a cafeteria worker—I still have a hard time believing what I've achieved. Six appearances in the Final Four. A national championship. NBA rosters studded with my former players. A short detour of my own coaching an NBA team. And in 2015, election to the Naismith Memorial Basketball Hall of Fame.

The weekend of my induction, I was surrounded by family— my wife, Ellen; our daughters, Erin and Megan, and son, Brad; my father and two sisters—and by friends, mentors, and former coaching colleagues. My mother, one of the greatest influences in my life, had passed away in 2010, but I felt her presence that day. (She always believed I was capable of anything; until the day she died, she believed I could be president one day.) What made it even more gratifying was the large group of former players, more than eighty of them, who traveled to Springfield, Massachusetts, for the ceremony. There's a beautiful picture of this, all of them gathered behind me—my extended family from the three college programs I've led.

The next morning, a big group of them got on a plane and flew to Kentucky to play in our annual alumni game to raise money for charity. Keep in mind that many of these young men were NBA players who were just about at the end of their off-seasons. Young multimillionaires on top of the world. They could have been spending the weekend anywhere—in South Beach, Las Vegas, the south of France—but they spent it with me in gritty Springfield and then back where we began together, on campus in Lexington.

It reminded me that it's not always the length of time you share that forms a deep bond, but the quality of it—what you can accomplish in each day that you're given. I'm far from done as a basketball coach, but this seems to me a good time to reflect, to share some of my hard-earned wisdom—and to think about how what I do applies to realms outside basketball.

This book, broadly, is about leadership, which in my mind is another word for teaching. With that in mind, at various parts throughout the book you will find small sections we've called "Beyond the Arc." When you are leading and working with extremely talented individuals—no matter the profession—you have to think differently. You have to think in an extreme sense. What do I need to do as the leader to bring out the best in this individual to help guide them to their dreams? Hopefully these sections prompt you to think, and maybe even act, differently.

Every day I'm with my team, I teach a game and a culture. I talk about what I believe our common values should be and I try to model them. I teach communication, team-building, and self-sacrifice. I introduce them to the concept of servant leadership—the idea that their satisfaction as players, teammates, and human beings should come from helping those around them succeed.

I do all this with extremely talented individuals who are, in some ways, less prone to believe they have to change. But when they can be convinced to surrender to coaching—if I can show them, as we say in our program, how to become "the best version of themselves"—the results are powerful.

In some ways, this is not a traditional business book. I'm a storyteller (as well as a person who enjoys hearing stories), and this is the story of the methods I have come to believe in after three decades in coaching—the reasons behind those methods, why they work, and how it all applies to anyone seeking to lead a winning organization.

SUCCESS IS THE ONLY OPTION

ASSEMBLING THE TALENT

A business executive by the name of Walt Bettinger likes to tell the story of the only course in college in which he failed to get an A. Bettinger, the president and CEO of the Charles Schwab Corporation, was in his senior year and really determined to keep his perfect 4.0 grade-point average. He had spent hours studying and memorizing formulas for a difficult upper-level business course.

The professor handed out the final exam and it was on just one piece of paper, which surprised everyone because they had anticipated a test with dozens of questions, as Bettinger recalled in an interview with Adam Bryant, author of the Corner Office feature in the *New York Times*. One side of the paper was blank and when students turned it over, so was the other side. The professor then said to them, "I've taught you everything I can teach you about business in the last ten weeks, but the most important message, the most important question, is this: What's the name of the lady who cleans this building?"

Bettinger had no idea and neither did the other students. He had seen her many times, but didn't know her name (it was Dottie) because he had never asked or even engaged her in conversation. He was a titan on the way up, a talented young guy ready to conquer the world. Maybe he had mumbled a "hello" to Dottie or nodded in her direction but that would have been the extent of it.

He failed the exam, the first time that had ever happened to him, and got a B in the course, ruining his perfect academic record. But as he tells the story, it taught him to be open to the world rather than having tunnel vision. He has made it a point never to look through anyone, even someone who's doing what is often considered "menial" work.

When Bettinger interviews candidates for jobs, he doesn't inquire much about their qualifications or skills. He knows they would never have made it all the way up to his level for an interview if they did not have the proper technical abilities. Instead, he tries to get a sense of their human qualities. What was their greatest failure? How did they respond to it? Do they seem to take personal responsibility or lay the blame elsewhere? If he's meeting a job seeker for a meal, sometimes he'll even get there early and ask the waiter to mess up their order a bit. (He promises a good tip in return.) He just wants to see how candidates react to this mild level of adversity. Do they say anything? Are they flustered or even rude?

One reason I like what Bettinger has to say is that he doesn't downplay the importance of talent and pretend you can just throw together a bunch of really high-character people and get the job done. At his level of business, I'm sure that's not the case. He needs top performers, just as any enterprise does if it wants to compete at the top level in its field. If you want to make a basketball comparison, it's the same reason you'll sometimes see a No. 16 seed in the NCAA tournament play with incredible spirit and give a No. 1 seed a real scare. The crowd goes crazy. Everybody in the arena who's not a fan of the highly favored team is rooting against them, hoping for a historic upset. The underdog team gets close but never wins.

To extend it a little further, it's why the teams that make it into the Final Four are usually made up of the high seeds. If a low seed sneaks in, it is often a top program with a core of elite athletes that has had a bumpy season, like Syracuse last year. Or sometimes like us, in years when we've been underseeded—like 2014, when we made it to the national championship game as a No. 8 seed.

Talent matters. There's no way around it. But the gold standard is to get your talented team to play with the desperation of one of those No. 16 seeds. The players on your team must be closely connected to each other, which means they must have human qualities. They cannot be robots. They have to see one another and truly care about the other person.

Bettinger needs high achievers, young people just as brilliant as he was. But he understands that it's not enough—it's just one part of the equation. He is also deeply interested in how his people will work together on teams, whether they have the ability to empathize with each other and the customer.

I don't pretend to know how to run other businesses, since I've been in my current one my whole adult life. But I do know that as basketball coaches, we are responsible for building and establishing success in fast-paced, high-pressure environments. We've got highly talented, ambitious individuals who have to give up a little of themselves for the greater good. More so than ever, what I do—working at speed to build closely collaborative teams—mirrors the challenge faced by leaders in the business world.

There's a term used in the high-tech world these days to describe people who back in my childhood we probably called "brainiacs." Or maybe if we were being unkind, "nerds." They're now known as "smart creatives" and they are much cooler now: They're running the world and inventing a lot of the stuff we carry around and depend on, like our smartphones and all the apps loaded onto them.

Significantly, these people no longer work in isolation. The stereotype of the inventor alone in his lab, if it was ever true, no longer is. The smart creatives pool their intellectual capacity because it's understood that is the best way to create success. "As commerce becomes increasingly global and complex, the bulk of modern work is more and more team-based," the bestselling business author Charles Duhigg wrote recently. He referenced a *Harvard Business Review* study that found that "the time spent by managers and employees in collaborative activities has increased 50 percent or more in the last two decades." In many workplaces, high-level employees spend the majority of their days together on teams, which is why the fancy new corporate headquarters are designed with very small private offices, if they have them at all—and lots of common areas. The idea is to get people to come together and collaborate.

The same article stated: "Within companies and conglomerates, as well as in government agencies and schools, teams are now the fundamental unit of organization. If a company wants to outstrip its competitors, it needs to influence not only how people work but how they work together."

In sports, we love to use military language. We go to war with each other and for each other. We have each other's backs. We look after our brothers. If someone gets hurt, it's next man up. We probably overuse these terms, to tell you the truth, but the reason we speak like that is that we understand the value of shared responsibility. We don't have to wait for quarterly reports, studies by consultants, focus groups of our own employees, management shake-ups. We live it every day. Everyone in sports has experienced very directly the power of coming together—and the consequences of coming apart.

Basketball is unique among sports in that we ask our most gifted players (our own "smart creatives") to do less than they are capable of—take fewer shots, score fewer points, don't keep the basketball in your possession too long even if you're the one most capable of making a play with it. We don't limit our players' creativity, put them in boxes, or, in business-speak, wrap them in layers of management. They are their own managers while the game clock is running. I think that's one reason why basketball coaches are sometimes listened to on matters of leadership. The people we lead are empowered—a frequent goal in the corporate world.

Basketball is a game of free will—players, in the course of a game, make moment-to-moment choices and come together and share for the common good, or not. The guy with the greatest talent can assert it at a maximum level on every trip down the court, or he can calibrate what his team needs. There are some models to follow, to an extent: The classic "pass-first" point guard, for example, shares the ball through the first part of the game in order to get everyone involved, but if he has dominant offensive skills, he may choose to take more shots at "crunch time" late in the game.

It's up to me to try to teach the kind of decision-making that in real time—in the course of the game—occurs in fractions of a second. I am trying to change instinct, habits. To give one example, I had to just about beg Derrick Rose to shoot the ball more. I've had plenty of other players whom I had to convince to attempt fewer (and better) shots. Jamal Murray became one of the most efficient players in college by the end of his freshman season. We were able to teach better decision-making, as well as the value of sharing the ball. Brandon Knight was another "volume shooter" in high school, sometimes putting up as many as forty shots a game.

By the time he left Kentucky, he became an efficient player who would make the big shot, as he did against Princeton and Ohio State in the NCAA Tournament.

Another study, this one at the Massachusetts Institute of Technology's business school, looked at the teams within corporations that worked best together. Now, keep in mind, these groups are all going to be made up of pretty smart people. Ivy League–educated, Stanford, and so forth. But even among these exalted individuals, you're going to have a few who are clicking along at a little faster pace than the others. They get it before the others do. They think their ideas are better and some will want to push them to the front so they get personal credit when the whole thing lifts off.

But this study showed that most successful teams—those that put the best products into the marketplace and made money for the shareholders—were the ones where people spoke in equal amounts. Everyone listened, even the brightest light. Team members took turns taking the lead.

That all makes sense to me. To have one smart person dominating one of these small groups would be no more productive than if my most gifted kid hogged the ball and took more than his share of the shots. What happens in that case is you shut down everyone else. You get 100 percent of the top dog's output but about 30 percent of what everyone else has to offer. It's a bad trade-off.

In the corporate world, the employees with an inclination toward collaboration are said to have a high "social sensitivity." They are not just smart and technically proficient but also gifted at knowing how others feel based on their tone of voice or social expressions. They know when to step back and when to come forward. It's not political correctness—it's what, in social settings, might be called manners. They know how to share and wait their turn. As one study put it, "They are sensitive to one another's moods and share personal stories and emotions."

Keep in mind, of course, that in my case I'm working with young adults or postadolescent males, depending on how you look at it. This isn't a slice of humanity known for its sensitivity to other people's feelings. (They're still trying to get a grip on their own emotions.) That comes later among young males, if it ever does.

My guys are athletes. Action-oriented. They are more physically than emotionally inclined. But basketball is the most social of all sports and the most intimate. Five teammates on the court at a time. A dozen or so on the whole squad.

I don't coach from up in a tower. I'm right down there with them. I've got to get them to notice each other, care about each other, take a step back at times, and sacrifice—because that's the only way we succeed.

Character Comes First

College coaches are often said to be in the "recruiting business," and fair enough—it's essential to our success. The same is true of anyone who runs a business of any size, right down to the guy who owns the local hardware store. He might be really smart about what he does—picked a great location, knows the right inventory and how to price it—but it's the people he's got in the aisles who make him or break him. That's his team.

It's not difficult at all for me and my staff of assistant coaches at Kentucky to put together a list of players we're interested in recruiting. Those names are well known. I sit with other college coaches in gyms and we're all looking at the same set of kids. There's maybe fifty or a hundred of them in each class—many who have been identified early on as rising stars and usually a handful of late bloomers who surged near the end of their high school years. We all have our favorites but the cream of the crop is fairly obvious.

There's no way we could be successful without getting our share of these players. We don't sign every one of them we want, though in every season at Kentucky we've been ranked as having one of the top incoming classes. On the flip side, we don't jump at a kid just because he's got the right physical attributes and skills. That's one of the great benefits of success. If a kid is interested in us but he's not the right fit, or if he shows me something I don't like, I can say "no," and I do.

Character always matters, but especially when you are dealing with young people who are counting on each other and can be influenced by their peers. I look very closely when I recruit to observe how players are to their teammates, coaches, and family members. A kid does not have to be a straight-A student (I wasn't) but does he do the best he can? Is he honest or is he always looking for a way out? (I'll write a little later about excuse-makers and blame-shifters.)

The other essential thing I am seeking is passion. I would tell anyone, "Chase something that you love." I would think this goes for any kind of business recruiting. If you're the senior partner in a law firm, you're not going to sit there and quiz the applicant about Supreme Court cases. He knows that stuff and so do all the other top applicants that get sent your way.

The job he's in line for is really hard, just like any job worth having. As an associate, he's going to work eighty-plus hours a week. He's gunning to become a partner and is in competition against a bunch of other associates. I'd want to probe and see if he has the capacity to find real joy in this work, even as hard as it's going to be. Is it stimulating—or just the means to an end? Does he love the work and the challenge or is it just the prospect of the big office and the salary that's driving him?

I want my players invested in the process, just drenched in the whole idea of learning their craft. Getting to that next step on the ladder is a powerful incentive, but if that's the only thing motivating someone it's never enough. The work itself has to be a reward.

I always ask my players: What's your why? Why do you want to have success? Is it just for fame and fortune, and if you attained that, who would it be for? When I get down past that first level, what I often hear is: It's for my family, or my mother. I've had one kid who said he wanted to build an orphanage in Haiti. I am more attracted to people who have a vision beyond themselves, because then their "why" is more powerful. What's driving them forward is a cause bigger than their own self-interest.

Human gifts and resources are unevenly distributed and it can seem downright unfair. But if you come out on the lucky side, you've got to understand your enormous good fortune and seize it. I don't feel like I've ever worked a day in my life, because through my college years, I got to play basketball, and right after that, I started coaching it. I've never stopped being grateful and never will.

A big part of my coaching consists of saying to my kids: You do understand how lucky you are, right? You have to be grateful. And that's not just one conversation. It's a version of what we're talking about every day. My players have not lived a lot of life yet so there's plenty of stuff they don't understand. A lot of them have aspects of their upbringings in which they legitimately don't feel fortunate. But what I know, from my adult perspective, is that they're hanging on to a winning lottery ticket—their extreme talent.

There's been a whole area of research lately about gratitude and its benefits across the board. If you're truly thankful, you sleep better, live longer, are more productive, have better relationships, and on and on and on—and I believe this wholeheartedly. What I tell them is that in order to cash in this ticket they're holding—and I don't just mean monetarily—they must acknowledge their gift and be truly grateful for it. Otherwise, they will never fully understand that they are walking around with something valuable, they stand a chance of squandering it.

When I'm recruiting, I'm looking for a kid who's alive. He's got a bounce in his step. A smile on his face. Love for his teammates. Jamal Murray, who played for me last year, is a great example. He came into the gym every day like it was Christmas morning. Big smile. Let's get started! He reminded me of my son, Brad. When he was about eleven, I'd say to him, "Who has more fun than you?" And he'd always answer me, "Nobody!"

I consider it part of my role as a coach to sort of monitor my players' moods and keep an eye on what I call their body language—what they are projecting to the rest of the world. Jamal actually looked after me in the same way. If I walked into practice without a smile, he'd say, "C'mon, Coach!" It would lift me up. How couldn't it?

People who followed us know Jamal had this bow-and-arrow routine after he made a three-point shot in a game, turning toward the bench like he had just hit a bull's-eye. If you're strictly old-school, you hate that kind of thing. I was fine with it except for the fact I wanted Jamal to immediately change directions after the shot went through the net and play defense—rather than going into his pantomime act. I'd be screaming and waving at him to run back down to the other end of the court and guard somebody, but I couldn't ever stay mad at the kid. He was too much fun to be around and too good for the group. His joy was infectious.

He came by it honestly. His father, Roger Murray, who taught him the game in Kitchener, Ontario, is as effervescent as his son. He cross-trained Jamal, starting with track and field (which was Roger's sport) and moving on to kung fu. He gave him basketball, at first, in small doses, but Roger says that it was like Jamal was "falling in love" with the game every time he set foot on the court. A couple of times he had to tell Jamal to try to quit smiling so much while he played because he was afraid it might be misinterpreted by his opponents as disrespect.

No basketball player can be bing-bing-bing all the time and bouncing off walls. The sport takes deep concentration. But if one of my guys is too exuberant or excitable, I can pull him in a little.

There's a spirit that Jamal had that many of my other players, like Michael Kidd-Gilchrist or Tyler Ulis, also possessed. You can see it and you can absolutely feel it. If it's not in there, I can't help a player find it.

Not every player can be like Jamal, but sometimes when a player looks downbeat, it's actually just a case of bad body language. He's not projecting what's really inside him. Lots of times, I can work with these kids and help them change. But if basketball is drudgery to you and I get that sense, I'm moving on. I'm running as fast as I can in the other direction.

If you walk into a gym and hear the ball bouncing and that doesn't get your heart beating a little faster, you're not getting anywhere in this game. Basketball is fun, man. You'd better show me you feel that way or I'm not interested in recruiting you.

If you're too hung up on your recruiting rankings and pedigree, there's a good chance you will open your doors to some people who are going to make your life miserable. Instinct has to play a part.

It's not scientific. It's from the heart and gut, which play a part in any industry.

BEYOND THE ARC

- Talent matters and it wins out. Don't ever fool yourself into thinking you'll reach the top just with a bunch of high-effort, high-energy individuals. They must have talent.
- Character matters. When hiring, you can never knowingly bring on people without character or who lack a spirit of collaboration just because they have extreme talent. You'll be sorry every time.
- Zero in on job seekers who are excited by the work and the process of getting better, and not just by the rewards (money, perks) or the prospect of career advancement. They have a passion for the job at hand.

A Lively Mind

I used the word *intelligence* a little earlier but another way to think about it is that I'm looking for lively minds. Ones that fire and respond—that absorb the information we're giving them and make quick decisions on the court and sound choices off it. Every business, every workplace, calls on people who have a combination of intelligence, knowledge, work skills, and social skills.

I don't need players who can qualify for Mensa, the genius society. Like I said, they don't have to be straight-A students. Some of my players come from inner-city schools, or systems in the Deep South that in most cases put them at a disadvantage. But there is a baseline. One of the greatest misconceptions of sports fans is that the athletes they are watching don't have to be smart. It's just not true.

I've had many players whose extreme drive on the court was matched by their work ethic in the classroom. Brandon Knight, for one, was a straight-A student, and even though he is not among the most physically overwhelming players I've ever coached, his intelligence has helped make him become an elite NBA player. When extreme intelligence is matched with extreme physical talent, you get superstars and possible future Hall of Famers—Anthony Davis, to give one example, or Karl-Anthony Towns.

I'll talk about curious minds later in the book, but players with curious minds need less motivation to be continuous learners. They need less of a push. They're in that mode. They want to learn.

We're all looking for people who are not slowed down by the group. They're always trying to think ahead and learn new ways. Stay up with innovations, so that they can be industry leaders.

The Relationship Between Passion and "The Grind"

The routine of building up your basketball skills and your body is what I call "the grind." It's everyday repetition in the gym and the weight room. A lot of drills and sweat. You're with your basketball buddies, or sometimes by yourself, while other people you know are at the mall, the movies, the big party everybody's talking about. These days, the party is on social media. You don't have to imagine what you're missing; you can see it. The grind is a lot of work but it only feels like work if you don't have the right passion.

I try not to use myself and my playing career as a model for any of my players now. Very little of it applies. It was a long time ago, another era. I got recruited to a lower-level Division I team (University of North Carolina at Wilmington) where I didn't get to play much, then transferred and had a pretty decent career at Clarion University in Pennsylvania, a Division II school a couple of hours north of where I grew up. I never had the size, speed, or athleticism of the kids I'm coaching now, but the one thing that did and does still apply is the grind. That has not changed. Whatever I achieved in high school or college ball, that's what it came from.

My house was right across the street from the high school. Every day I was in that gym, lots of times after hours when the whole school was closed up. I knew how to jimmy one of the doors and then contort my body—I was all of 150 pounds—to squeeze through an opening because there was a chain they put on to keep it from swinging all the way open.

Years later, the athletic director would say that someone had given me a key but that wasn't the case. I snuck in, though they probably knew about it. I'd practice everything—ball handling, foul shots, jump shots from different parts of the floor. And I kept at it day after day after day. I was driven to get better and to squeeze out every ounce of whatever measure of talent I had been given.

The grind relates to any kind of business you're in. When you're competitive, you work yourself to the limit. You push and then you push some more. On a really good day, I start tomorrow's work tonight.

When I travel for recruiting, I try to do at least four things a day: meetings at breakfast, lunch, and dinner, along with a late-night meeting. At the end of the day, in the hotel room, I'm sitting on the bed with my feet on the floor and I'm both exhausted and fulfilled. I've left nothing in the tank.

At Kentucky, our players live together in a small dormitory that's not more than one hundred steps from the front door of our practice gym inside the Joe Craft Center. That's by design. I want our players in there as much as possible, grinding to get better. They are on campus during the summer—for a stretch once school starts but before we start practicing—and after our season is over. My hope is that they spend long hours in the gym working on their games. They don't have to sneak in.

The other thing is, even in-season, a college kid's day is not a straight eight- or ten-hour shift. They have practice. They have schoolwork. They've got a lot on their shoulders, but it's not like they're putting in time at a steel mill or coal mine. A lot of them like to play video games, which is fine. They need downtime to unwind. But they have windows of time where they can walk across the parking lot and into the gym.

What they do over there doesn't have to be physically taxing if we're in-season and going hard in practice. But let's say one of my players is shooting 53 percent from the foul line. The night before, we had a game and he was a little off his average—he got seven foul shots and he hit three of them. Two of the misses weren't even close.

Can you tell me why you would ever be playing a video game instead of shooting free throws?

Michael Kidd-Gilchrist is one of those athletes who looks like he was chiseled from granite. That is the foundation of his extreme talent. A physique built for basketball. Six foot seven and 230 pounds of fast-firing muscle.

Michael was a ferocious rebounder and a ridiculous defender— one of the best I've ever had—able to guard any position on the floor. I'd put him on somebody and usually it was like making that player disappear, even if he was the other team's star. The other team had to go elsewhere for offense.

He wasn't the best outside shooter or the slickest ball handler and passer. He came to us as just okay in those regards, though he improved during the season and has continued to in the NBA, where he plays for the Charlotte Hornets. He was what I'd call a play finisher rather than a play starter. He was so good on the end of the fast break that I made a rule: If he was out ahead of the ball, you had to pass it to him, and if you didn't, I'd take you out of the game.

Michael's other essential gift was his extreme passion—his spirit and his appetite for work. I can't take any credit for that. He arrived with it. It was already in him. All we did was give him a place for it to flourish. But if I am looking for the prototype of passion, the type of young man I'd want to have on every team, it's Michael Kidd-Gilchrist. If I see that pure love of the game and fierce will to get better, combined with the right physical attributes, I'm reaching for it every time.

Michael knew about a tradition with the old Chicago Bulls in which Michael Jordan would gather teammates at his house early in the mornings before practices or even on days off for weightlifting sessions. Jordan's chef would cook for them, so they called it the Breakfast Club. Kidd-Gilchrist instituted the same thing with us in 2012, our championship season. Before class, there would be a bunch of our kids, more and more as the season went on, trudging across the parking lot and into our gym. They lifted weights and got out on the court and worked on basketball skills.

The great thing is, the story of Michael Kidd-Gilchrist and our own Breakfast Club has now been passed down from one Kentucky team to the next. Most of our kids know about it even before they get here. Every season since, we've had one kid who starts it. A few of our guys follow at first and then more and more as the season goes on, and the stakes get higher.

In the corporate world, they talk about building a culture. I think Michael helped us build a culture of passion. It's a bond among young men who have truly been blessed with extreme talent that they will all commit themselves to the grind and make the most of their gifts. We are trying to take the next step now to make it more about a lifestyle than just a culture because lifestyle entails twenty-four hours—not just when you're at the office or on the basketball court.

BEYOND THE ARC

- As the leader, you can model certain behaviors and aspects of your company culture but you are not the prototype. In most cases, you are going to be older, more established, and, in some ways, unrelatable to those under you.
- Highlight examples from within your workforce of the qualities you value, as I do: to give one example, as I've just done with Michael Kidd-Gilchrist.
- You have to learn to love the grind. Loving the grind and feeling fulfilled at the end of a hard day should be part of the culture that extreme talent embraces.

Be Willing to Be Surprised (or, How I Fell in Love with a Tiny Point Guard)

For most of basketball history, the majority of people who knew a little about the game would have said the most important position on the floor is center. The sport's history is rich with big men at that position who led their college or NBA teams (or both) to championships and, in some cases, dynasties. Their names are legendary: Bill Russell, Wilt Chamberlain, Kareem Abdul-Jabbar, Shaquille O'Neal, Bill Walton, Hakeem Olajuwon, David Robinson, Moses Malone. You would certainly put Tim Duncan on that list, too, though his position was often listed as power forward.

The assumption was that championship teams were built around dominant offensive forces in the low post—or in the case of Bill Russell, who won eleven NBA championships with the Celtics, an unbelievable defensive force. Either way, it started with a guy somewhere around seven feet tall.

The game has changed dramatically for a few different reasons. Part of it goes back to Michael Jordan, who won six championships in the 1990s with the Chicago Bulls. At six foot six, he was normal-sized by NBA standards. His position was shooting guard, or sometimes small forward. Can you even name the centers on his championship teams? There are some pretty devoted basketball fans who probably can't. For the record, the guys who played the position most frequently were Bill Cartwright, Will Perdue, Luc Longley, and Bill Wennington. It's fair to call them journeymen, though Cartwright did make it into one all-star game. They were all rugged defenders and rebounders, but it's not hard to imagine Jordan's Bulls winning the same number of rings with any number of other big men holding down the position.

The game has continued to evolve in other ways, post-Jordan—with the most important change in recent years being the greater emphasis on three-point shooting. Players are spread out all over the court, and some teams even go for long stretches without a traditional center on the floor. Officiating has changed at both the professional and the college levels, with "hand-checking" on the perimeter called very closely—which makes it harder and sometimes even impossible to stop a small, quick ball handler from getting to where he wants to go.

Without the ball being pounded into the post on every possession, decision-making is more important at every position, but the biggest responsibility falls on the point guard. Coaches have always put a high value on that position. Start with the fact that a whole lot of us were point guards. The point guard is the extension of the coach on the floor. If you think of it in terms of a computer, the point guard is the operating system—the thing that must function properly or nothing else works.

Teams with shaky point guard play tend to have problems that cannot be overcome, no matter how strong they are in other areas. They can't get the ball into the hands of the right players. They turn it over too much. In high-pressure moments—close games on the road, opposing crowd going crazy—they can't find a sense of calm. For a coach, there is nothing more unsettling than having a point guard you can't trust. You're always one step away from chaos, and there are only so many timeouts you can call to get everyone calmed down and reorganized.

I don't recruit in a certain order and say, for example, that first I'll get my point guard, then I'll fill in with a shooting guard, a small forward, etc. That's not practical. But I know it's the one position I have to get right. I've had teams without a traditional small forward—and as recently as last year, one without a strong post presence. I don't prefer it, but I can always think of a fix. A workaround. That's not the case if I've got a deficiency at point guard. (It's probably one reason why there have been years that we have two or even three high-quality point guards on the roster; I just play them together.)

I can rattle off some of the characteristics I want in a point guard: First is his ability to lead and to make others want to follow. Is he a true servant leader? (I will explain later what I mean by that term.) He must have a "tight handle," meaning he can control the ball on the dribble and protect it from defenders, and court vision—he sees the whole floor and spots open teammates. And I want him to have an ability to score. I don't normally go for a pass-only point guard, because one who is also an offensive threat—and able to score from the outside or drive strongly to the hoop—opens up the floor for everyone.

As for physical characteristics, let's just say that the point guards I've sent on to the NBA were pretty big kids. How many times have you noticed those whippet-quick point guards who are great in the open court but easily get trapped in a corner and they have to call a timeout—or they don't call one and the ball gets ripped away? Sometimes you can't even see them because they're buried in a thicket of bigger bodies. That's why I usually prefer a point guard who is able to see over a defense and is strong enough to withstand defensive pressure and physical play.

John Wall, Derrick Rose, and Brandon Knight were all six foot three or taller; Eric Bledsoe was a little shorter, at six foot one, but really solidly built. The starting point guard on our Final Four teams in 2014 and 2015, Andrew Harrison, was six foot six and about 220 pounds. Before he worked really hard and got leaner between his freshman and sophomore years, he looked like a tight end on our football team.

Which brings me to Tyler Ulis. When I say be willing to be surprised, what I mean is that a leader should always be open to challenging his own assumptions. Recruiting is one of the most important things you do. We all have prototypes in our heads—the perfect specs for a given job. Has to have the right qualifications, the experience and pedigree. But sometimes those prototypes have to be thrown out the window because talent can come in a different package than you might expect.

When my staff gives me the names of the high school players we should be looking at, kids Tyler's size are never on it. If I'm out recruiting, it's not unusual for me to take an interest in a player who's not already on our list. He shows me something and we'll start following him. But even then, to be honest, I'm usually going to look right past someone like Tyler. He is (charitably) five foot nine. We listed him at 160 pounds, a weight I think he might have hit after a big bowl of pasta and two helpings of ice cream. The last time he was officially weighed the needle hit 149 pounds, so he is like the size of an eighth grader.

I always said that if I was ever going to recruit a kid like that, he would have to be a freakish athlete. A pit bull with a motor that never quits and a jumping bean that can put his nose on the rim. But I was thinking of a kid who's maybe six feet even. At our level of basketball, that's my idea of small.

Tyler could not put his nose on the rim and I'm pretty sure he's the only scholarship player I've had at Kentucky who could not dunk. (I'm told that he could throw it down if someone threw the ball up there for him, but I never saw it.) But he had those other attributes—the motor and pit bull mentality—and much more.

He played for Marian Catholic High School in Chicago. I first saw him when he was an eleventh grader. On the dribble, he pounded the ball so hard and so low to the floor no one could ever take it from him. He was pass-first but he could shoot it out to three-point range, and if the game was on the line, you could count on him to hit it. He was developing a "floater"—the very difficult shot in the paint, almost a cross between a layup and jump shot—that little guards must have because they can't power the ball all the way to the rim. If they get by that first line of defense, they need to stop short and shoot the floater rather than challenge the big guys guarding the rim.

NBA players sometimes cannot hit that shot with any consistency until they've been in the league for several years, and have spent their summers perfecting it. It takes long hours and thousands of repetitions to get the right touch. Seeing Tyler's ability with it let me know that he had spent hundreds of hours by himself practicing that and other skills. He was a gym rat, driven by his passion to improve and a chip on his shoulder that came from an obvious place: People had always dismissed him because of his size.

On defense, he was a constantly disruptive force. An irritant. He always picked up full-court and would dog the other team's ball handler so relentlessly that the kid would struggle to get over half-court in the allowable ten seconds. If the offensive player was careless with the ball, Tyler picked his pocket. And these weren't overmatched opponents—I'm talking about scouting Tyler in AAU games against other highly ranked players who were made absolutely miserable by his energy and determination.

The other thing I loved was his utter fearlessness. Like all our recruits, Tyler came to campus right after his high school graduation to start classes in the summer. The new players bond together and end up playing pickup games with former players, who often visit as they round into shape for their upcoming season. In a story that has become almost legendary among Kentucky fans—but is, nonetheless, true—Tyler got in a scrap one afternoon with DeMarcus Cousins, who is six foot eleven and 270 pounds. (So that's a foot taller and one hundred pounds heavier.)

Words were exchanged, followed by some pushing and shoving. Before cooler heads broke them up, Tyler was ready to fight De-Marcus. That's a little crazy, but a good kind of crazy. The point guard is the leader on the floor. Who wouldn't want to follow a kid with Tyler's stones? You might be afraid not to.

When we signed Tyler, a lot of people said, "Good, now you've got your point guard for the next four years." The thinking was that at his size, he would never be NBA material.

Our program is for the highly advanced: Every scholarship player has that potential to play pro basketball and every one of them wants to. The reality—and I'll discuss this at length later—is that the NBA dips into the freshman class for most of its high draft picks. Their next preference is sophomores. The longer a player stays in college, the less attractive he is to league executives. I don't necessarily agree with it because everyone is on their own timetable, but that's just a reality my players have to know.

When people said he would be with us for four years, because he did not have NBA size, I told him, "If that's how you feel don't come here." It's not that I wouldn't want to keep coaching him, but I never want my players crimping their ambitions. Whatever the highest step on the ladder is, I want them trying to get there.

Tyler was the backup point guard, but in name only, to Andrew Harrison on our 2014–15 team. He played 23 minutes a game and was usually on the court in the crucial last minutes, often with Andrew. He stayed for his sophomore season and his importance to our team was such that he almost never left the court—he averaged 37 minutes and several times played the full 40. (It's unusual for any of our kids to average much more than 30 minutes.)

Tyler averaged 17 points a game with 7 assists—against just two turnovers, an extraordinary ratio—and all his numbers got better as the season got later and the games bigger. In our SEC conference tourney final, when we defeated Texas A&M in overtime, he had 30 points and 5 assists. He played all 45 minutes and turned the ball over once. Any basketball fan knows those numbers are completely ridiculous. No one plays 45 minutes of a pressure-packed game with the ball in his hands most of the time and loses it just once.

Every drill we do is intended to enhance players' decision-making. We do high-energy, high-speed stuff where they have to make quick decisions under duress. We talk about "fast feet, slow mind"—by which we mean that they must be able to, with their eyes, slow down the action and make proper choices. It's a version of the same thing that any business confronts. There are times when things are moving very quickly and you're facing an array of choices. You must make the right one, and quickly. You're operating under stress, at speed. There are businesses that make a point of recruiting college athletes, and I understand why. The best of them have a calm under pressure that is rare. Tyler excelled at all of these drills. He set the pace and the standard and his teammates followed.

He piled up the postseason awards: first-team all-American, winner of the Bob Cousy Award, which goes to the nation's top point guard, player and defensive player of the year in the Southeastern Conference. He set the school record for most assists in a season, breaking John Wall's mark, and posted other numbers that had never been achieved before at Kentucky, among them the most games with at least 20 points and 10 assists. He was the shortest consensus all-American since 1958. I called him the best court general I had ever coached—a pretty big statement considering I've had point guards go on to win MVP and Rookie of the Year awards in the NBA.

What Tyler did for me was widen my own horizons. I'm not necessarily going out looking now for five-foot-nine kids. But I'm definitely not looking past them, either. I got a laugh out of what Chad Ford, ESPN's draft prognosticator (and one of the few who knows his stuff), wrote about Tyler: "Ulis is small—but, man, can he play."

Seek Out Risk-Takers

It takes a certain kind of courage for a player to choose our program. You have to want to bang up against teammates in your own gym who are your equal—understanding that on some days you won't come out on top. You know you'll be in a dogfight for playing time. We've had McDonald's all-Americans who struggle at times to get on the court.

Recruiting is always, in part, a risk. I make a judgment that a player's skills and athleticism will translate to this higher level of play, but does he also have the aptitude to quickly learn the new stuff he'll need? Does he have the right character and is he a good fit? Can he thrive under the bright spotlight that shines on the Kentucky basketball program and deal with the high expectations of our fans, who are known collectively as Big Blue Nation? Does he truly love playing basketball? I feel like I have been right on the vast majority of the kids we award scholarships to, but you can never be 100 percent sure until you have them on campus and the games begin.

The other side of the coin is that the player I recruit is taking a risk. Another coach recruiting the player may say: Come with us and I promise that you'll start, play 35-plus minutes, and get 20 shots a game. You'll be the face of our program. We'll round up a great supporting cast for you! We'll put guys in your orbit, complementary types, to make you look good.

This can be an alluring option and what might seem like a safe choice. I don't pretend these decisions are easy. Some kids want to be the unquestioned star at a program they hope to elevate— maybe get it into the NCAA tournament if the team has not been a regular participant, or deeper into the tourney if it's been going out in the early rounds. If this doesn't happen, though, some of the blame may even fall on the player, unfair as that may be, and it can affect his future. (If he's so good, why didn't the team do better?)

I don't make any guarantees to players I'm recruiting, and I would say to any of them: Why on earth would you want one? Don't you want to feel that whatever you accomplished, you earned? You own it because it didn't come in a promise. I tell kids up front that they will have to compete for playing time. The message is very clear: YOU ARE RESPONSIBLE FOR YOUR OWN SUCCESS. If you want a guarantee, go to Popcorn State. You'll play as much as you want and get to take all the shots.

I want boldness and what I call swagger—a strong self-confidence that edges up to but does not cross the line into arrogance. Swagger means that you believe you can be dominant but know that you have to work to achieve that status.

The whole guarantee thing has a larger life lesson wrapped up in it, and it's one that extremely talented people in any field need to hear. They've had success and praise all their lives. They naturally feel the applause will keep on coming. Making promises just amplifies the applause. The leader has to turn the volume down on that. None of us has a guarantee we're even going to be here tomorrow.

To tell them exactly how something is going to set up for them six months or a year down the road isn't fair. I can't know for sure what's going to happen, and even beyond that, if I give them a guarantee I'm not giving them something but actually taking something away—which is their opportunity to go out and earn it. If you hand athletes something, they'll never have swagger.

But we do talk about results. More than 68 percent of our players who have finished their college careers at Kentucky have been drafted into the NBA, and that includes walk-ons. (Without walk-ons, it's 76 percent.) We have had the number one pick three times at Kentucky, and fourteen lottery picks. We have sent forty-one players to the NBA during my stops at UMass, Memphis, and Kentucky. One thing that's really remarkable is that of the twenty players who left after just one year with us, half have averaged more points in the NBA than they did at Kentucky. We didn't hold them back. They learned the value of sacrifice and sharing in our program, and carried that forward into their pro careers. At the same time, their scoring blossomed. It is the best of both worlds.

When I say the players in our program must compete for court time, I fully expect they will thrive. If I didn't think so, I would not be in their living rooms. It's not a process of attrition where I bring in a group and figure that a couple of them are going to fail. I expect them all to succeed. But it's not easy. If I have eight or nine guys who deserve to play, those are the ones who get minutes. If I have six, that's the number I play. If you're not among them, you'd better battle it out at practice to get yourself game time.

I never write a kid off. We coach everybody in practice like he's a starter. But I'm not going to put you on the court just because I feel sorry for you.

The depth of our typical incoming classes may scare off some kids. And I can never be sure how many kids from the previous season are coming back. It can get crowded, and everyone knows that. The ones who choose us are fearless. There are others—some of them just as talented—who turn and walk in another direction, and I'm okay with that.

Talent Flocks Together

In any business, opportunity attracts talent. A corporation, a law firm, or even a university trying to lure a coveted young professor might put a lot of money on the table. But ultimately, those in the most highly gifted segment of the workforce want to be with their peers. They crave internal as well as external competition. They need to be pushed. It's in their DNA. They are looking for mentors and competitors and an environment where they can grow. These are the people who you want on your team and who will propel you to the top.

I was on a phone call with a recruit who talked to me about his aspirations and his dreams. When I got off the call, this came to my mind: If you walk in a gym and you're the most talented one there, you're in the wrong gym. If you walk into a gym and you look at the talent and say, "Wow!" you're in the right place.

In previous eras of college basketball, you had your upperclassmen host the kids you were recruiting. They were potential teammates. That is not as much of my focus now because the kids may never be on the same team with so many players leaving early for the NBA. I have high school players I'm interested in visit at the same time, and to a large extent, they recruit each other. Certain ones decide they want what we have to offer and they start bonding together before they even arrive.

In my business, our currency is playing time. Players (and sometimes even more so, their families) regard it as highly valuable. It's how everyone in the game comes up, craving what's known as "PT"—playing time. First you want to make the team—and then you want "starter's minutes." If someone is "taking your minutes" it's like he picked your pocket. It's all part of the culture of our sport, and it's so ingrained that many players do not even like sitting out when we're practicing.

The regular season in college basketball is thirty games. In only about twelve of those games are you likely to be playing against a team with future NBA players on its roster. If your goal is to be a pro, those are your opportunities to be judged by scouts against top-tier competition. If you don't have a depth of talent on your own team—players at your level to compete against in practice—those dozen games may be the only times over the course of an entire season that you bump up against your peers. That's a maximum of 480 minutes—from October through April—that you are pushed and accurately measured.

In our program I have to get people to think differently and understand that it's the quality of the minutes you get in games, not the quantity, that matters. Players at Kentucky do not usually play thirty-five minutes a night, though, as I said earlier, there are occasional exceptions, like Tyler Ulis. It's rare for us to have a volume shooter.

But how about if every day you come to practice, you're matched against another potential pro? You're telling me that twelve games are better than that? We don't have a "second string." If you're six foot ten and 230 pounds, you're not practicing against a slightly built player five inches shorter; you're probably facing a kid in your own gym who is your mirror image, or close to it. If he's a little smaller, he might be quicker and more skilled and you've got to deal with that. The impact of that is monumental. You get two hundred days of growth.

Here's another example. We have had Dominique Hawkins in our program for four years. Our fans have a special feeling for him because he's local—he was Kentucky's Mr. Basketball in high school and led his team, Madison Central, to a state championship. He was also a football star.

At six foot even and 190 pounds, he is an unbelievable athlete—very strong with great quickness and an explosive vertical leap—but especially in his first couple of years, he was a notch below most of our other players in offensive skills. But he's a killer on defense, so much so that in his freshman season he logged important game time in our run to the national championship game—including eleven minutes in the regional final against Michigan because I needed him to defend its best scorer, Nik Stauskas. (Dominique barely touched the ball on offense because we never passed it to him, and he did not attempt a single shot.)

With his offensive game still evolving, Dominique has been in and out of the regular playing rotation, but he is fully present every day at practice. The result is that our other guards have to go up against an NBA-quality defender every time they're in our gym. When he's on you, you're being guarded, and it's a battle. In very few games on our schedule will our other guards compete against somebody harder to score on.

Two years ago, we had four players who were lottery picks in the NBA draft. One of them, Devin Booker, did not start a single game. Think about it: 39 games coming off the bench, and he was the thirteenth pick in the NBA draft and is already on his way to being a future all-star. None of the players on that team averaged more than 26 minutes a game. Karl-Anthony Towns, who would become the top pick in the whole draft, averaged 21 minutes, barely more than half the game.

In 2011, Enes Kanter was the third pick overall in the whole draft. He not only didn't start a game for us—he didn't play a single minute. The NCAA ruled him ineligible, unfairly, I believed, on their unproven suspicions that he had received benefits to play for a pro team in his native Turkey. He was allowed, however, to practice with us.

The NBA's Utah Jazz selected him based mostly on what their scouts saw of him in our gym—in practice.

BEYOND THE ARC

- Recognize how your industry is changing and adjust your recruiting accordingly. An applicant who may not have fitted your specifications in the past may very well be a good match now.
- Understand the mind-set of highly sought recruits. Are you selling them on the value of personal growth—and the value of working with other extremely talented, highly ambitious peers?
- You can never guarantee job seekers that they will succeed, especially when they are entering a highly competitive environment. What you are selling them on is not the assurance of success, but your confidence that they have the tools to thrive and that you have the expertise to help them do so.
- Talent attracts talent. The best want to be among their peers.

2

KNOW THE RED FLAGS

have red flags in recruiting, stuff that leads me to just walk away. A big one is disrespect. If I'm in a kid's house and he disrespects his mother or his grandmother or any member of his family, I'm not dealing with that guy. I can't. I don't have time.

Any leader has to know his own limits, what he can change in a person and what he can't. I can sometimes change behavior but I can't change a person's essential character. Respect is something that gets instilled. You're raised with it. I feel sorry for a kid who doesn't have it, but I don't have a quick cure for him. If I take him into our program, then it's likely that he won't respect his coaches, his teammates, or the values and goals of our program.

Another red flag is if a recruit has shady characters around him. I'm not talking about the grassroots basketball scene, which is populated by all kinds of people—a majority of whom are good and well-meaning, a few you're not sure about, and then some who are just bad apples. If any player I recruit comes from that world I'm not going to penalize him for it because of somebody in his orbit or background whom I might have doubts about. But if these types are in his inner circle and he's listening to them—or if he consistently makes bad choices in who he associates with—that's another story.

It's the same thing with bad choices. If he has ten doors he can walk through—nine of them are really good and one's bad—but he keeps finding his way to the bad one, that's defining. I hope he goes off to college and changes, but it's not going to be with my program.

The world has gotten smaller, in a way. It makes it even less likely a kid will leave his problems and associations behind. Those people from his past are in his cell phone. To an extent, they're in his head. They can get on an airplane and come visit. I can't build a wall around my basketball team and keep all that stuff out. If I try to save this one kid, I might end up letting in influences that are going to have an impact on us all.

In the recruiting process, you're better off being honest with yourself and losing him to another program. You might even have a moment of doubt and think, darn, I could have changed that kid. But it's probably a fantasy. There are times I imagined myself a Father Flanagan, thinking I could save anyone, and realized it was not possible. Nothing can screw up a potentially high-performing team more surely than adding the wrong person to the mix.

Almost every year, I'm able to say that I love my team and they're great kids. Those aren't just words for the media; I mean it. I don't coach Eagle Scouts or angels—believe me, they're young and capable of doing dumb stuff—but I try my best to weed out those who are just not going to be able to stay on the right path.

Avoid Blame-Shifters

Refusing to accept blame and shifting it to others is about the worst trait you can have on a team or in any work environment. I don't know that you can coach around it if it's really ingrained. You can be super-talented but if you've got that as part of your character, it might be fatal.

This is my opinion based on three decades of coaching, and one shared by experts who have studied interactions in the workplace. Nathanael Fast, a management professor at the University of Southern California, has written, "Playing the blame game never works. A deep set of research shows that people who blame others for their mistakes lose status, learn less, and perform worse relative to those who own up to their mistakes. Research also shows that the same applies for organizations. Groups and organizations with a rampant culture of blame have a serious disadvantage when it comes to creativity, learning, innovation, and productive risk-taking."

What's even more alarming is that blame-shifting is apparently contagious, like a virus. Fast's study on that, written with another professor, Larissa Tiedens of Stanford, has a fancy name— "Blame Contagion: The Automatic Transmission of Self-Serving Attributions"—but the syndrome he describes is not hard to understand. It boils down to: I point my finger at you for something that was my fault, you point at the next guy, and he turns around and points at someone else. Soon enough you've got a whole group of people pointing at each other.

Some call this the "victim mentality." (It can't be my fault because look at me, I'm the victim of this thing that just happened.) What results from this is a "culture of fear" in which people are afraid to take chances or to make mistakes. Everyone just crawls into his own bunker. If you asked me to describe the opposite of the culture I wanted to create on my team, that would pretty much be it. Paranoia. Finger-pointing. Everybody looking for a place to hide.

A big thing I look for is how a player relates to his teammates, coaches, and even the referees. I imagine that it might be difficult, in a way, to recruit football players because it's harder to get a sense of their personalities from watching them play. They're wearing helmets. It's a big field and you're probably pretty far away. You'll get a sense of their speed and technique—and probably even more of one from watching their film—but to know something about them as people has to come from elsewhere.

As a basketball coach, I'm in the bleachers, usually in a pretty small gym. I can see their faces. I can see—and often hear—their interactions. I get an up-close observation of a player and learn something about him beyond just his athleticism and skills.

If he's on an island by himself, I see that. It's clear to me that the only thing he's worried about is his game and his stats. When he does something good, he sprints back on defense, claps, has emotion. He's really happy. When he thinks he's open and a teammate takes a shot rather than passes to him, he glares. If he's got the ball on the bounce and snaps off a good pass to a teammate but the kid fumbles it out of bounds, he's got a look on his face again. You can read what he's thinking: C'mon, man, that was my assist.

If you can't attract top-tier talent, you might have to take that guy. You hope you can change him or you tell yourself, "I'll get that out of him." It could be possible, but I'm fortunate not to have to take the chance.

Basketball character and actual character are not unrelated. It's one of the great things about our sport. You can get a read on a person's personality by his mannerisms on the court.

Bill Walton, the former UCLA and NBA great, said of Tim

Duncan, after Duncan had played what looked like it could be his final NBA game after twenty seasons: "He personifies everything I believe in—in basketball and in life. I don't separate the two." There's really something to that. Basketball does reveal character. I think it would be almost impossible to be a bad human being and a truly good teammate.

Let me put out a couple of caveats about blame. People in general are not always great at accepting responsibility, and few of us start out being what we adults call "accountable." Who among us can't remember a moment when we made a mistake and looked around and hoped no one noticed? You walk away from the window you busted with a baseball and hope nobody finds out it was you. You leave the milk out overnight and you're okay when your little brother takes the heat for it.

Truly owning up to our mistakes is a learned behavior, a part of growing up. I've got young men who are still in that process, so it's my job to continue to teach them. They come from all kinds of backgrounds, including maybe some where they were not secure enough to admit to their failings. It could be that being wrong wasn't an option because the consequences were out of proportion. I've got to recognize that and make allowances—but only up to a point.

I've also had a few kids who have almost the opposite problem, like Derrick Rose, who was too hard on himself. He had a weight on his shoulders. Anything that went wrong, he'd say, "My fault." I had to say, "Derrick, that wasn't you. Stop beating up on yourself."

Every player is different and their ability to truly take responsibility depends on their experiences from home. How they've been raised, how they've been treated, how they've been coached. Were they enabled—and did they therefore come to believe nothing is ever their fault? Were they beaten down to the point that they came to fear they wouldn't amount to anything?

Or are they just stubborn, what I'd call hardheaded? They've got a ton of confidence and come from a background of pure success. These types of kids are usually smart. They don't pass blame but you've got to go extra hard at them to convince them that something needs to be fixed.

Karl-Anthony Towns flirted with that at times. If I wanted him to defend the pick-and-roll one way and he did it another, he might say to me, "But that's the way we were doing it yesterday." Right, but this is how we're doing it today. Karl's first reaction, especially early on, was often "What, me?" but he never pointed his finger at a teammate and blamed. I can work with that, and I did.

And Karl, I should add, was smart enough to find a way to deal with it himself. He invented a character, sort of an imaginary friend, who lived on his shoulder and whom he named "Karlito."

Karl was such a great kid that he didn't want to talk back to me, so he would cock his head and talk to this little guy. Or sometimes he'd berate himself after he missed a free throw or a close-in shot by taking it out on his imaginary friend. I had no idea at first what he was doing until someone told me, "Coach, that's Karlito."

QUESTIONS TO ASK A JOB APPLICANT OR RECRUIT

- Tell me about a bad decision or choice you have made in your life.
- When did you realize you had made a mistake?
- What were the consequences?
- Did you accept them or fight them?
- How did you correct your mistake?
- Did you ever make that same bad choice again?

A Profile in Accountability

In 2012, we defeated Kansas, 67–59, in New Orleans in the final game of the NCAA tournament. It was my first national championship and the program's eighth. I have, of course, thought about that game many times in the years since—and I've talked a great deal about the performance of our freshman center, Anthony Davis.

But now, almost five years removed from that game, and thinking about some of the issues addressed in this chapter— accepting blame as opposed to shifting it; the nature of true accountability—I am even more impressed by what Anthony did that night. He set an amazing example in how to deal with adversity.

He made just one field goal, which came in the second half with about five minutes left in the game. Overall, he was 1 for 10. Keep in mind that on the season, Anthony's shooting was better than 62 percent. Over the previous two tournament games, he had taken 17 shots and made 13 of them. He had very little experience on how to respond when his shots weren't falling, and now here he was, in the national championship game, less than a month after turning nineteen years old, and he's dealing with something new.

When things go bad, a gifted player—and by gifted I mean in both talent and approach to the game—will adjust and pivot. The other guy will blame. He'll look at the ref and beg for calls. His body language might suggest that the fault lies with his teammates. Maybe they're not getting him the ball in the right spots or not passing it to him as soon as he comes open. The player who blames looks for exterior reasons to explain his struggles; he doesn't look within himself.

Anthony never blamed, nor did he sulk or get down on himself. He came in at halftime that night and said, "I can't make a shot.

I'm done shooting. I don't know what's happening, but I will rebound every ball and block every shot. You guys do the rest."

I preach to my teams all the time: What are you doing when you're not scoring baskets? I said to Anthony in the locker room at halftime, "Don't worry about it. You were the best player on the floor without scoring a point." And that wasn't just to make him feel better. It was true.

Anthony was voted the game's most outstanding player, and I'm pretty sure that even if the NCAA title game is contested for the next one hundred years—or let's say two hundred years—there will never be a winner of that award with his stat line. He finished with 6 points (four foul shots in addition to his one basket) but dominated the game in every other facet with 16 rebounds, 5 assists, 3 steals, and 6 blocked shots.

We were a very balanced scoring team to begin with, but his teammates responded to Anthony's leadership ("You guys do the rest") by taking care of the offense. Doron Lamb led us with 22 points and two others scored in double figures.

ANTHONY DAVIS ON BEING RECRUITED BY COACH CALIPARI

When I was coming out of high school I felt like I would be a starter at whatever program I chose, but Coach Cal walked into my living room and said it's not something you can just count on at Kentucky. At that point in your life, everybody's been making a pretty big fuss over you—they all want you to sign with them—so it took me back at first. And then you consider what he's said and you gain respect for him telling you that. Right away, it gives you something to work for.

The other thing is that it brings the team closer together. When you all get on the court, you know that everybody is fighting and earning their spot—the new guys and the ones who have come back. When everything gets established, you never feel like, "That guy over there is playing for X reason; that other guy is playing for some different reason."

Nobody got promised playing time. We've all been in a war together and know that the guys in the starting lineup and the ones coming off the bench have rightfully earned their spots.

It gives you respect for your teammates and your coaching staff and the team. It feels good, because you have that foundation of regard and respect for each other. We call our teammates our brothers, but it's not just a word. It feels like that's who we are to each other because we're in the experience together. We've all fought it out and then come together as one team.

BEYOND THE ARC

- How do you promote accountability in your workplace? You make sure you're accountable as a leader. You must show before you teach.
- Do you model it as a CEO or manager and take responsibility when you could have done a better job yourself? (If you are a blame-shifter, you can be sure everyone under you will follow your lead.)
- When someone steps up and is accountable for a sale that was lost or some other initiative that came up short, how do you respond? Do you use it as an opportunity for the whole group to come together and figure out how to get it right the next time?

3

UNPACK YOUR BAGS

t's one of the first things I tell players when they get to campus: Unpack your bags. I don't care if we're together for just one season—meaning eight months from the beginning of practice in September until our last game in late March or April—or for two, three, or even four years. Take your underwear and socks out of the suitcase and put them in the top drawer. Put your T-shirts in the next drawer down. Hang your pants and good shirts in the closet and find a place in the room to display some family pictures.

We have a beautiful campus and quality academic program. Our kids have been very good students during my years at Kentucky, averaging better than a 3.0 grade point average in almost every semester. They start summer classes on campus beginning right after they get out of high school, and most who stay for a while either graduate in three years, or come close. (Alex Poythress played his senior season in 2015–16 while taking graduate courses.) Every single one of my Kentucky players who has stayed four years has graduated. Our recent Academic Progress Rate, a measurement of the NCAA, put us in the top 10 percent of all Division I schools in men's basketball for the second consecutive season.

But there is always that other thing on the horizon—pro basketball, "the league," as we call it—and I understand that's why they came to play for me. That's their goal and we never pretend otherwise. Because most of them have been identified at such a young age as gifted, it has always been about the "next thing" for them. It often begins with high school coaches recruiting them as soon as they hit middle school, if not before. If they're not already playing for one of the top AAU teams on the circuit (or even if they are), some other club is always trying to grab them. From there, it becomes: What college will they choose? And then, even before they play a single game at Kentucky, it's the NBA, with the Internet full of "mock drafts" predicting where they'll land when the league makes its selections in the spring.

Are they lottery picks? Maybe the top pick? Once the season starts, the question becomes: Are they moving up the draft board, slipping down, or even, God forbid, falling all the way out of the first round? They're going to click on it no matter what I say. I tell them all, I don't want you to plan on staying for just one year. Think about two years, at least. They settle in that way; they take care of business academically. If you're that good and you can go to the NBA after one year, and that's what you want, fine. I'll back you.

But there comes a moment in life when you've got to stop looking so far down the road. Be fully present where you are, for however long that is. I don't care what field you're in. For young people, and particularly for those blessed with extreme talent—for whom there is always going to be some great new opportunity up ahead— it's the only way to grow. You must be still for a period of time. Reflective and receptive. In learning mode.

If you get caught up with what's supposed to happen in eight months, nine months, or a year, it's overwhelming. It causes anxiety because you're reaching for something that's too far away to touch. People talk about one-and-done. How about one day and done? What challenge did I take on today? What did I accomplish? What was the most important thing I got done?

My players have rarely been in a grouping with their equals. But now they are being challenged—in the same way any other highly gifted person would be in a classroom or workplace of their peers. They have to stay right in the moment and learn how they measure up, and how to handle that.

Anyone in this situation must have a coach, a mentor, or some kind of leader who can say, Here's the deal. You've got work to do to be considered among the best at this level, let alone the next one. You can get there, and it's in you, but you need to do the following things.

Creating Joy

In any organization, there are certain foundational principles that should be stressed right from the start. From the moment my players arrive, we talk about the concept of how we create joy in our lives. True joy, I tell them, comes from being a giver. On the court, among their teammates, when they are off the court and out in the world, I want every one of them to be a person who lifts up others.

We talk about joy every day and when there is an opportunity to make a difference off the court, we seize it. I want my players to know that their great gifts come with responsibility. They can do more good than the average person. Several years ago, our kids were on the phones taking calls in a telethon to raise money for victims of a devastating earthquake in Haiti, and we raised more than

$1 million. Our team did the same in the days after Hurricane Sandy, which flooded communities in New York and New Jersey.

I noticed afterward that my players had a different bounce in their steps, just by the connections they made with other caring people on the phone and the difference they were making in the lives of people they would never meet.

We have consistently had players who leave us for the NBA and quickly give millions of dollars to charities in their new cities—and back home where they come from. I'm talking about money from their first contract, not accumulated riches they give late in their careers. They have won and been finalists in the awards that the league gives to players who have made the biggest impact off the court. They have embraced being servant leaders, a concept I explain in greater detail later in this book.

I will tell you, selfishly, that the good we do off the court is also good for our team. It makes our kids better teammates. It takes their own burdens off them—whatever their day-to-day concerns may be—because they have turned their attention to people with far greater struggles.

I believe that you finish the way you start, which is why this fundamental principle of ours—create joy—is introduced right from the start, as we unpack the bags. I want them to know that Kentucky basketball is about more than the dozen or so guys wearing the uniforms. We have a lot of people we can help. To fail to reach out and do all the good we can do is like missing a ton of foul shots—it equates to just wasting opportunities. I want them to enjoy the college experience, and thoroughly be engrossed in all that goes along with being a college student. They are not the normal student, so they have to handle themselves differently. But they can still stay in the now and enjoy being on campus.

What I really enjoy is when former players come back and talk about their experiences and what they've learned after the fact.

Willie Cauley-Stein just came back and said, I wish I had spent more time in the gym; I'm going through that process now. And he told all of our guys that. He was being a mentor, just as Karl-Anthony Towns was a mentor to Skal Labissière—and in the same way that Eric Bledsoe reached out to Isaiah Briscoe after Isaiah announced he was staying for his sophomore season. Eric told him: You've got something to prove now.

BEYOND THE ARC

- True joy comes from being a giver. How do you give back? Your job is about more than just doing the job. You have a responsibility to others. It gives you purpose.
- How you start is how you finish. Teach your people from the beginning that they are responsible to each other and to their community.

Settled In? Okay, Now It's Time to Get Uncomfortable

My job is to push each of these players through his comfort zone. In the weight room, you'll hear, "No pain, no gain." I must make each of them as uncomfortable as I can in practice daily and in individual workouts, stretching them to the limit so they discover what their limit really is.

Karl-Anthony Towns was seven feet tall by the time he came to us in 2015 for his freshman season. He was not quite as explosive an athlete as Anthony Davis, who is just an inch or two shorter, but he had other attributes. Karl moves his feet very well and has long arms, soft hands, and elite hand-eye coordination. He had been a baseball pitcher and also played a bit of golf, and if you watched his comfort level at handling the basketball—shooting it, passing, dribbling—you could imagine him doing those other things. There is a natural grace about him that you don't see in many athletes his size. (Just so you know, Karl played in our celebrity softball game for charity this past summer and hit a slow-pitch softball out of a minor league ballpark.)

Off the court, he has the same ease about him, a comfort in his own skin. He was elected class president at his high school in northern New Jersey, and he's the type who could have been chosen "most likely to succeed" even without being a basketball player. His high school grade point average was over 4.0, when weighted for his honors classes, and he talked of becoming a doctor, as he put it, "after the basketball goes flat." He came to Kentucky because he liked the kinesiology program, which was his major and what he plans to continue studying as he finishes his degree.

His father, a high school basketball coach, drilled Karl in fundamentals. There were weeks that he only let him use his left hand to shoot, so he could be an offensive threat going in either direction. Karl's mother is a native of the Dominican Republic, and I first spent time around him when he was sixteen years old and I was coaching the Dominican national team. He was in ninth grade and six foot ten. His teammates were professional players either in the NBA, like Atlanta Hawks all-star center Al Horford, or in various international leagues.

Karl's talent was obvious but he liked to roam around the perimeter, near the three-point line, rather than going down low and mixing it up with the big guys. In high school games, he attempted a ton of three-point shots and hit for a decent percentage. When he got to Kentucky, that was still his inclination. The finesse game. It was pretty to watch and it would have helped us plenty; after all, players who can shoot the ball from distance are always welcome.

But I wouldn't accept it. We said, "You're going to get in the post you're going to learn to battle." There have been big players in the NBA, six foot ten and up, who are good outside shooters but shy away from the physicality down low. They never amount to as much as they could. And then there are guys like Kevin Garnett and Karl Malone, excellent jump shooters who were also skilled and relentless around the hoop. Even Dirk Nowitzki, a seven-footer and one of the best three-point shooters in NBA history, has terrific post moves. If the other team tries to defend him with a smaller player, in order to chase him off the three-point line, Dirk posts him up down low and scores that way. He's got sharp elbows and a tough mind-set.

Malone is in the Hall of Fame and Garnett and Nowitzki will join him the moment they're eligible. That's the future I envisioned for Karl, but I knew I had him at a formative moment. A window can close on young players. The danger is that they will achieve what may feel like a high level of success without ever having to reach down and develop all aspects of their games. They might even become all-stars, but they'll never be Hall of Famers or centerpieces on a championship team.

An eighteen-year-old like Karl cannot be expected to grasp the full dimensions of his potential, so I function like an early warning system: Here's what I see inside you. And here is how not to let it go to waste. It's not that I have a greater ambition for a player; I just may have a better road map.

The key for all of them is to build from strengths while also developing new parts of their games. I don't want them to try things in games they are not capable of, but once they've developed some proficiency, you can't be scared to do it in a game.

Each summer I tell them, "Each of you should figure out ways to make yourself a little uncomfortable. Work on different parts of your game in pickup games. In other words, in some games you're looking for drives, in other games you're looking for jumpers. Some games you're looking to post up, other games you're looking for pick-and-pops. Some games you're not going to shoot any balls because you're going to be concentrating on creating for your teammates. Challenge yourself with one-dribble pull-ups or pull-ups in transition. If you're not uncomfortable, you're probably not improving."

I let Karl know from day one that I wanted him to get down on "the block"—the area just outside the three-second lane, close to the basket. He would have to learn how to establish position, make himself available to properly receive a pass, and operate with his back to the basket. Proper footwork would get him a short jump hook, sometimes a dunk. He'd be in position to get offensive rebounds.

An oddity of basketball is that you want to have tall players, but they must "play low" with their butts down and their feet spread wide. The competition down on the block isn't glamorous. You bang with your opponent. He drips sweat all over you. At the end of the game you've got bruises—or sometimes even stitches if you catch a stray elbow. It's a dogfight every night, and just to survive, you've got to get in the weight room and toughen up.

I mentioned that the modern style of basketball is now more wide-open, with shooters spread out all over the floor. In some ways, that makes a player like Karl even more valuable. If he's a threat down low, he'll find less "traffic"—fewer big bodies—to contend with. Because he already had advanced court vision and passing ability, he could find open teammates when he was double-teamed, but no one would need to put two defenders on him unless he showed fight near the basket.

Karl was invested in being a nice guy. Great, I'd tell him. I love being around you. Everybody does, and hold on to that. But it can't be your persona on the court. I'm never going to accept anything less from you and just shrug it off and say, "Oh, that's just Karl being Karl."

Playing low on every trip up and down the court is physically demanding, and he wasn't ready for it. His legs and core weren't strong enough at first to hold his position. To compensate, he resorted to using his upper body and elbows to move opponents and clear space for himself, and there were games early on in which he spent a lot of time on the bench with me because he got whistled for early fouls. Other times I had to sit him down because he wasn't fighting. He would get pushed off the block or he just drifted off on his own, back to where he was comfortable, and looked for jump shots.

That 2014–15 season was one in which we were absolutely stacked with talent. We platooned two five-man squads until we lost Alex Poythress for the season with a knee injury, but even after that we played nine and sometimes ten guys. We were bigger than most NBA teams, with two other seven-footers—Dakari Johnson and Willie Cauley-Stein. In most games, we could survive without Karl for stretches if we needed to.

A game at South Carolina sticks out in my mind as a turning point for Karl. It was mid-January, so not all that early in the season, but he was still catching on to how we wanted him to play. That's normal; it always takes time. I'd see flashes of what I wanted, then he would revert. He made two of his three shot attempts that night, missed both his foul shots, and grabbed a grand total of one rebound.

I never leave a player on the bench as punishment, but it's only fair to keep the kids out there who are doing more. Our platoon system only guaranteed minutes to players who were battling. He played just twelve minutes that night.

After the game, I saw Karl's parents. He probably had rarely struggled much at anything before, and I knew it wasn't easy for them to watch. I normally try not to talk to parents about basketball (I'll engage them on almost anything else about their child) but I made an exception. "I'm not letting up," I told them. "He's going to be unbelievable by the end, but I'm not letting up on him."

His mother said she thought he was fighting better in the post. "No, no, no," I said. "He's not battling enough. You want him to shoot threes? Nope, sorry, I'm not letting him go out there." I then hugged her and kissed her cheek.

I was forcing Karl to do stuff that was uncomfortable. It wasn't that he didn't want to, but his body and mind were not habituated to that level of intensity. He was such a big kid and fluid athlete that in the past there was no place he wanted to get to on the court that anyone could keep him from, nothing he wanted to get done that anybody could really prevent. He could score inside or outside, whichever mood struck him. His coaches were always delighted.

It wasn't just post play he had to learn. On defense, I was teaching him to guard pick-and-rolls, the most difficult skill—and increasingly, one of the most important skills—for any big man. With the professional game more wide open, and shooters spread all over the court, a big player has to be able to compete around the hoop and jump out on smaller players to either prevent open three-point shots or impede them if they try to drive to the hoop. Our team needed Karl to learn that and Karl needed it for his future.

I mentioned that our seasons are short and we have to make fast progress. Sometimes Karl didn't seem to realize that. He could be almost too thoughtful for his own good, like he was dreaming up reasons to take baby steps. He told a reporter during the season, "It's almost scientific. When you try to make something grow quicker than it's supposed to grow, it doesn't come out right. It's not as good. "

Really? That was news to me. One thing that really helps is that my former players often come back to campus during the summers and work out with our current ones. They get to know each other and continue to text and talk. Around midseason, Anthony Davis, on a day off for the New Orleans Pelicans, came around to visit. He had a sit-down with Karl and basically told him, "Hey, kid, you'd better step on the gas here."

Anthony had been through the same process. In the beginning, everyone said, "He's talented, but wow, if he was only tougher and had a post game. What would that look like?"

Anthony had grown late in high school. He had guard skills, which was good, but I didn't want him to have a guard's mentality. He wasn't resistant, and neither was Karl, really, but they needed to get stronger and get down low and see the benefits. Ultimately, it's about experiencing some success. You want them to feel that, build on it, and then own it. After that, it becomes not what I want for them but, instead, part of their competitive identity. They embrace it as their own.

I believe in stating our intentions publicly. Say them out loud, and hold a player accountable for what you believe he can achieve. If that equates to pressure, it should be a good kind of pressure. I told the media (echoing what I had been telling Karl privately) that by the end of the season, I thought Karl would be the best player in college basketball. If he chose to leave us and enter the NBA draft, which I knew was likely, I wanted him to be the first overall pick.

That may have sounded unrealistic to some people. There was another player who everybody thought had the first pick locked up. And Karl was playing only about twenty minutes a game for us because of the platoon system, and sometimes less because of fouls. He was still learning—but he had stepped it up and was catching on fast.

BEYOND THE ARC

- It is the leader's responsibility to tend to a young person's development, and this is especially true when you are leading extreme talent.

- Understand the difference between "accepting" certain behaviors and letting an employee know that there are certain things you expect but that he is not yet capable of and therefore must add to his skill set.

- Be wary of early and easy success—the kind that comes to talented people just because they are blessed with more resources. You must let them know that as the competition gets more intense and the stakes get higher, it will become more difficult for them and they will have to build more capacity. Prepare for new competition to enter the marketplace.

- Understand that building more skills can be a foreign concept to gifted people because they've always prevailed with the ones they already have. The good news is that once you can convince them that they have more to learn, they can often do so more quickly than the average person.

Turning Setbacks into Growth

Young people continually build skills, piling them up one after the other as they move toward mastery. Their mental approach—to school, athletics, work, household responsibilities—is less of a steady march of progress. There are lapses. Two steps forward, one step back. Any parent knows that. You look at your kid sometimes and think, Wait a second. You just did WHAT?

It's the same deal with my team of postadolescents. As I've written, our season goes by very quickly. You can imagine it as one of those time-lapse videos, superfast-forward, but it's not exactly that. We take little steps backward, too. Basketball, more than most sports, is a free-flowing, unpredictable game. You've got to be able to read the game and respond correctly. Off the court, it might be called reading social cues. What subtle thing just occurred? Do I recognize it? Even though there's no script for it, what's my response? What's the one thing that is definitely the wrong response, the thing I can't do? Maturity matters and so does hard-earned wisdom that you gain only from making mistakes.

I'm going to stay on the subject of Karl a bit longer because his season with us demonstrates so much. Not only was he gifted, but he was so self-possessed that I could throw a lot at him. One of my credos is "Coach your best players hardest," and I was never afraid to do so with him because I knew he could take it.

Another model of the same thing is Gregg Popovich and Tim Duncan of the San Antonio Spurs. Pop often said that a big part of his team's success was that he could coach Duncan, one of his best players, as hard as or harder than anyone else.

With Karl, I had him over to my house one day and told him, "I'm going to be harder on you than anyone, because you have more of an upside. Understand that I love you and that I have one thing in mind—to get you to be the best version of you." And he said, "Coach, I'm in." It was even more important that year that I could coach a star player in this fashion because we were going to play the platoon system, two five-man rotations, and everyone had to give something up. The players had to feel they were all in it together, equally. I told Karl that if it ever got to be too much for him, to come talk to me, but he never did. He listened, wanted to learn, and valued my instruction. I never had to worry that anything I said would shake his inner core of confidence.

In February, a couple of weeks after the South Carolina game, we played at LSU. It happened to be my birthday, and by the end of the night, I felt like I had aged two years. I tell our kids every year that when you play for Kentucky, we're everybody's Super Bowl. We get the "white-outs" with everybody in special T-shirts, and the ESPN College GameDay with all-day parties leading up to tip-off. But my kids can't fully understand until they experience it.

We were 23-0 entering the LSU game, and a capacity crowd inside the Pete Maravich Assembly Center, the first sellout there in a decade, was at a fever pitch from the moment we got on the court for warm-ups. It got so loud that you could understand why it's often called the "Deaf Dome." LSU was good, with a couple of future NBA players, Jarell Martin and Jordan Mickey, on its front line. They got off to a lead early, but we settled in and with about ten minutes to play in the second half, had a 60–52 lead. That might not seem like a lot, but this was the best defensive team I had ever coached and when we were really dialed in, which was most of the time, an eight-point lead could feel like a pretty comfortable cushion.

Andrew Harrison, a sophomore, was an experienced point guard who did not turn the ball over. Tyler Ulis, in his first year, was the other point guard, but at the end of the games, when we had both of them in, it allowed us to really control tempo and made it awfully difficult for teams to come back on us.

I'm pretty sure we would have coasted home except for what happened next: Karl lost control of the ball as he went up for a dunk and could not complete it. He then hung on the rim and did a chin-up—like he was doing a pull-up in an eighth-grade phys ed class. He might as well have shouted: "I may have missed that dunk, but watch this!" What he should have done after fumbling the ball was just run back and play defense, but it was like he had to tell everybody, "I'm into me now." The chin-up was an automatic technical foul, and it was called. It totally reversed the game's momentum.

I took him out of the game and went crazy on the sideline. Maybe not my finest moment but I had been through some of this before with Karl, as I had with many other players over the course of my career. Sometimes they think they're out there alone and it's all about them. They don't realize that there are just two kinds of basketball plays: winning ones and losing ones. (Or maybe a third category: utterly boneheaded ones.)

I had said to Karl at times during the season, "You don't play to win. You're just playing ball. You're just trying to show stuff." Sometimes he would make a pass or take a shot and it was like there was no game going on out there—no scoreboard, no clock, no nine other players. His blunder gave LSU new life and started them off on a run of 16 straight points.

People in the arena and watching on TV could see me gesticulating on the sideline. I wasn't mad at the official; I was absolutely livid with Karl. He took a seat on the bench and probably hoped I would walk away, but I had my back to the court and was in his face. I shouted, "I hope we lose! I hope we lose so you learn your lesson and you can deal with that!"

I also refused to call timeout to break LSU's run. I was like, no, let this thing go on. Let's see how bad it gets. I didn't really want to lose, but my larger point was: Let's really feel this. Let's understand the consequences. We can survive a loss, but I sure don't want to lose in the postseason because of something stupid like this.

It was a point made for Karl, of course, but coaching your best player harder is also a lesson for your whole team. Bad as it would have been if we lost, I knew Karl could take it. We all could. It would be a somber plane ride home but we'd regroup and move on.

I put Karl back in after a few minutes. No one's talent should feel like a burden, but it is a responsibility, and that is how Karl responded. He knew he had to dig deep into his reservoir of skills and do something. In the game's final minutes, he had a steal, an offensive rebound, a blocked shot, and baskets on a step-back jumper and then jump hook—all in quick succession. After almost causing us to lose the game, he won it for us. We squeaked by, 71–69.

It was a turning point for Karl. He grew up a lot that night.

'll get back later to our 2014–15 season, which was an experience like no other in my coaching career. We reached 38-0. But for now, the epilogue of the Karl story: At the NBA draft in June at the Barclays Center in Brooklyn, he was indeed the first name called, by the Minnesota Timberwolves.

A point of pride in our program is that we do not just send players on to the NBA: They are prepared when they get there. In almost all cases, they not only meet but exceed whatever projections were made for them.

Karl had one of the finest rookie seasons in NBA history. He averaged a "double-double"—18.3 points and 10.5 rebounds a game. He was among the league leaders in numerous categories—scoring, shooting percentage, rebounds, and blocked shots. He became one of only six players who at twenty years old had a game with 35 points and 10 or more rebounds—the others being Shaquille O'Neal, Kevin Durant, Carmelo Anthony, Chris Webber, and LeBron James. He played all eighty-two games and instead of fading as the season wore on, as often happens—players unaccustomed to the long NBA season are said to hit the "rookie wall"—he just kept getting stronger and better. After the all-star break, he averaged almost 21 points a game.

And yes, he took some three-point shots, almost one a game (I guess he earned the right!), and hit a pretty good percentage. He'll be a serious three-point threat in the NBA, but I already knew he had that in him. I was trying to give him the other stuff. (He attempted just eight three-point shots for us the whole season.)

I try to keep my eye on our guys who have gone on to the league as best I can during the season, watching parts of games and some highlights. One of my favorite moments involving Karl was one that probably a lot of people missed. The Timberwolves were playing the Golden State Warriors and Karl—playing defense against an unbelievable offensive team—got caught in a pick-and-roll and had to step out and guard a much smaller player: Steph Curry.

So, basically, he's thirty feet from the hoop chasing a guy a foot smaller than him—and one who is pretty much unguardable by anybody. Curry looks at Karl and takes what's called a jab step to make him back up, but he holds his ground. Curry then puts the ball on the floor, dribbles behind his back, changes directions, and makes his way from out beyond the three-point line to the right baseline.

At about ten feet from the hoop, he goes up for a shot but can barely even see the basket because Karl's still there, with his long arms draped over him. With the shot clock running out, Steph shoots an air ball. It misses the iron by a good two feet. It could be Curry's worst miss of the season.

I loved what Karl told the writers after the game when he was asked about this particular play. He said he enjoyed the challenge, which is one of the things I constantly preach: You have to enjoy this stuff. Enjoy the privilege of the fight even if you don't come out on top.

The next time Curry finds Karl on him, I'm pretty sure he won't be as surprised at how difficult it is to shake him—and he's unlikely to shoot another air ball. It wouldn't surprise me if he ran Karl in circles and then made him look silly with some kind of dipsy-doodle reverse layup. But I'd expect Karl to enjoy that, too, in his own way and start thinking about how he'd guard Curry the next time.

Karl was selected unanimously as the league's rookie of the year, and ESPN placed him on its third-team all-NBA squad, putting him among the top fifteen in the league—an extraordinarily rare accomplishment for a first-year player. He was one of just six players to play in all eighty-two games and capped his first NBA season ranked 8th in the league in rebounding (10.5), 8th in field-goal percentage (.542), 6th in total blocks (138), 26th in scoring (18.3), and 3rd in double-doubles (51). His 51 double-doubles in the regular season were 30 more than any other rookie's. The first time he played against Kevin Durant, then of the Oklahoma City Thunder, Durant said, "He's going to be a Hall of Famer in this league."

BEYOND THE ARC

- Are you willing to speak the truth to your most talented performers? Tell them exactly what you expect and hold them accountable. If you can't do that, nothing you say to anyone else will have meaning or impact. The people under you are constantly weighing your words and your tone.
- A reprimand or an aggressive correction must always be followed with an almost immediate opportunity for a person to redeem themselves.
- Basketball provides these instant opportunities for redemption, but nearly any business does as well. If a person is worth having with your company, you don't sideline that employee for long. You put them back in the game in order for them to show the best version of themselves.

KARL-ANTHONY TOWNS ON STAYING IN THE PRESENT

The best advice Coach Cal gave us was, "Play in the present, because it goes by really quick." The time did fly, but I used the time as wisely as I could. I became a much better player in the low post. Defensively, my IQ became better. I've been able to make the moves and not always have to use my height as a getaway car. That doesn't work when you get to the higher levels of basketball.

Playing fewer minutes than we would have elsewhere wasn't tough because we all knew about it from the beginning. We knew what the job was. We had so many good players, and we got to compete against each other every day in practice. We wanted to go there and we wanted to win and we knew that if we gave ourselves up, we could be good. And we were good—we were great. We didn't finish the way we wanted to, though.

All of us players, we leave Kentucky but it remains with us. I record every game they play, and I watch and root for them.

When I got to the NBA, I thought it would be more grueling on my body and on me mentally. I didn't realize how ready I was thanks to Kentucky. I had the mental capacity and also the physical strength to play at a high level, and I had the work ethic. That gets instilled into you by Coach Calipari and the coaching staff.

The Past Is the Past

If young people sometimes get ahead of themselves by rushing the future, those of us who are their elders have the opposite problem. We look to the past and have a tendency to dwell in it, talking about the good old days and how much better they were.

The American economy has changed in lots of different ways,

as most people know from their own experience. Employees don't stay with one company or even one career for a lifetime. You'd better put money in a 401(k) or an IRA because you're probably not going to get a pension. Books like *Free Agent Nation,* which was published more than a decade ago, envisioned a society in which everyone is sort of on their own—each person his own boss and his own brand.

People in their twenties now stay in one job for less than three years, and estimates are that they will have between fifteen and twenty jobs over the course of a lifetime. In Silicon Valley, where some of the brightest minds gravitate, the average time in a job is even shorter. I've read that when the most coveted software engineers keep one job for too long, they are not admired for their loyalty. Just the opposite, in fact. When they decide to finally leave, it can be difficult because recruiters wonder why they stayed put.

I can't say if all this is good or bad. It's probably a mix. But what I do know is that these changes are a reality. They constitute the world we currently live in, and in my business—in any business—it never does any good to complain about what has been lost and what's never coming back.

I need to stay current to be effective at what I do. A lot of people have probably seen Drake at our games. Jay-Z is a friend of the program, too. Does that help our recruiting? It might in some small way. Knowing a little bit about my players' world certainly can't hurt. (Just don't ask me to rap out any of their lyrics; I wouldn't be able to.) But it's also the way I'm wired. I'm constantly looking forward, not back, and our program reflects that. I don't actively go out seeking celebrity fans, but our program is forward-facing—as any business, educational institution, or even charity has to be—and those with the same outlook are attracted to it.

Being about the new takes many different forms. I was recruiting a player who was doing hot yoga as part of his training program. I didn't know what that was but I found out about it. After our 2014 season, I said to Ray "Rock" Oliver, our strength and conditioning coach at the time, "Let's take it up a notch." We've always been good in the summer, but we had that core of returning players, so I figured, let's mix it up and give them something new. They did some hot yoga and our track coach, Edrick Floréal, worked with some players on their legs and mobility. We had several players whose body fat measurements came down dramatically. Overall, our team was both leaner and stronger.

You'll never hear me saying how much better life was back in the day. First of all, in so many different ways, it's not true. The best time in history to have been alive is right now. There was a time when college basketball operated in its own little space. It had a core of enthusiastic fans but the whole thing was much quieter and more modest. Games were not widely televised, not even the NCAA tournament, and coaches found their best players close to home, often in the same state. It was the same great game but that's what it was: a game.

Like it or not, we're both a sport and an industry now and we connect to all the trends and changes in other parts of society—whether in education, business, or child-rearing. We're a globalized sport because it's a globalized world.

For decades, we had only a trickle of international players who made an impact on the game, but no one would say that now. To give one example, the dominant NBA franchise of the last decade, the San Antonio Spurs, has been led by a trio of players, the "big three," all born outside the continental United States—Tim Duncan of the U.S. Virgin Islands, Manu Ginóbili of Argentina, and Tony Parker of France (and born in Belgium). It's rare now for any good NBA team not to have a player from overseas among their core group. Maybe there are critics out there who lament that and figure we're losing American jobs, but any basketball fan can see that the foreign players have changed and enriched the game. In 2015–16, I had a player on my team from Australia, another from New Zealand, one from Haiti, and two from Canada. I had never had so many international players, but the sport had changed. I could either keep up or get left behind.

Just like other areas of life and society, college basketball has become more dynamic. There is less of a sense of permanence. I was twenty-nine years old when I got my first coaching job, in 1988 at the University of Massachusetts. They had been pretty good in the years back when Julius Erving played there, but when I took over, UMass was on a streak of ten consecutive losing seasons. They were not in a major conference, and ranked at nearly the very bottom of some three hundred major college programs.

I know that lots of people just assume that I've always been a hotshot recruiter, able to attract top-level high school talent, but it's not the case. It wasn't possible at UMass. In my eight seasons there, which included a trip to the Final Four and another to the Elite Eight, I had just one player who would make a career in the NBA: Marcus Camby. (Another player, Lou Roe, was drafted early in the second round of the NBA draft, then played briefly in the NBA and for many years overseas.) Marcus was among the most physically gifted guys I've ever coached—a relentless, six-foot-eleven shot blocker with a long wingspan and great leaping ability. As a classic "rim protector," he was an obvious NBA player, and yet he stayed with me for three seasons before declaring for the draft. That was the norm back then. A lot of talented players stayed all four years.

I liked having Marcus for that long a time, and in general I enjoyed coaching players for multiple seasons. But did I like it better? It may seem hard to believe, but I don't ever think in those terms. That world is gone.

'—————

've been viewed by some as the "one-and-done" coach, and I won't spend too many words writing about that. People will think what they think. But let me just say that I didn't invent or advocate for a system in which so many of the best players stay for just one year of college basketball before turning pro.

What we have now is something that came about as a result of wrangling between the NBA and the players' union (along with a group of powerful agents) after a period in which kids were allowed to go straight to the NBA from high school. A handful of them were so immensely talented that it worked out fine—LeBron James, Kobe Bryant, and Kevin Garnett, to give three examples. But others were not close to ready and they were wrecked by the system and ended up without satisfying pro careers or college experiences.

The NBA didn't like taking players out of high school because they could never be sure what they were drafting. And they had a hard time getting ticket buyers excited about a kid people had never heard of. Playing even just one year at a top college program makes a kid more recognizable and marketable. But agents, generally speaking, want kids in the league and collecting paychecks as soon as possible.

What they hashed out is the system we have now: one and done, for the majority of the top college freshmen. It is an imperfect compromise, at best. If you asked college coaches if this is the system they would design—your best players leave after one year and you have to reload each fall with a half-dozen or more new kids—I don't think anyone would say yes.

I have sent 41 players on to the NBA in the course of my coaching career, including 28 in just the last seven seasons at Kentucky. Four have been the No. 1 overall pick—John Wall, Anthony

Davis, and Karl-Anthony Towns at Kentucky and Derrick Rose at Memphis. In 2010 Kentucky became the first program to have five players chosen in the first round, and in 2012 we became the first school to have two players selected with the first two picks in the draft (Anthony Davis and Michael Kidd-Gilchrist).

People will say that I've benefited the most from recruiting one-and-done players but I say it's a hard way to coach. You're on a high wire every fall wondering what your team will look like and there are never any guarantees. You're starting over.

I look at myself in the mirror and sometimes feel like I'm aging two years for every calendar year. But the reality is that I accepted it before a lot of other people did. I didn't look backward—nor did I look forward with some unrealistic hope that the rules would go back to the old way. We're never going back to a system in which the top kids stay four years, and I don't think we should.

What I decided was the following: Every player we sign has a lifetime scholarship. They can come back at any time and finish their college degree. I'll say it again: Our scholarships are for life. You can come back anytime, and we want you to. That seems like a fair deal for everything our players contribute to the university and all the joy they bring to the commonwealth of Kentucky, which dotes on our program like no other fan base anywhere in America.

BEYOND THE ARC

PRACTICAL STEPS FOR STAYING IN THE PRESENT

- When you wake up in the morning you must ask yourself the question, "What's the most important thing I must do today?" Before you go to bed you must ask, "What were the most important things I did today?"
- Find a daily place of peace, away from it all, to collect your thoughts and remind yourself of who you are apart from the fast-breaking tensions of your workplace. For me, it is daily Mass, and when I can manage it—even during a break of a day or two during the season—getaways to the beach in Florida with my wife. For you it may be a daily routine of exercise, thirty minutes spent reading, or dinner with your family every night—no matter what other pressures are bearing on you.
- Connect with at least one person each day who has nothing to do with your work life. Consider it like a fifteen-minute vacation. It might be a good friend, a mentor, or perhaps one of your kids who is away at college.

4

KEEPING IT REAL

I n September 2015, Jordan Spieth, the talented young golfer, was playing at a tournament in Atlanta. He was near the end of one of the great seasons in the history of golf, having already won two major championships and five tournaments overall. At twenty-two years old, he was ranked number one in the world and had earned more than $20 million in prize money and probably millions more off the course in endorsements. But after carding consecutive bogeys, he fell out of the lead and was hanging his head a little bit.

At that point, his caddie, Michael Greller, who was thirty-seven years old and a former elementary school teacher, turned to Spieth and told him to snap out of it. "No more talking about anything that just happened," he said, trying to pull Spieth out of his funk and get him focused on the remaining holes.

Greller, as quoted by reporter Karen Crouse of the *New York Times*, explained later that his blunt talk to Spieth was typical—or maybe even a little milder than usual. According to Greller, Spieth will sometimes tell him, "'You need to yell at me.' He'll tell me in so many words that I've got to grab him by the head and get his head right. It's weird. It's like your boss telling you to yell at him."

When I saw this, I thought: how remarkable. Here's this young man absolutely on top of his sport and on top of the world. He is already rich beyond belief. It would be understandable if he took his foot off the gas at the end of a long season. No one would blame or criticize him. But he has someone walking the course with him whose role it is to not let him do that.

I'm sure there are a whole lot of people out there who can lug a golf bag, give accurate yardages, and help read putts. But the bigger a guy like Spieth gets, the more he needs someone in his circle to keep him honest—and he is smart enough to seek that out. The caddie knows Spieth's own high standards and he holds him to them. No wallowing, no mental letdowns. If you're at the tournament, don't play just to finish somewhere near the top and collect a paycheck. Play to win, which means showing the needed mental discipline.

There are so many lessons in this. One is that Spieth, an extreme talent by any definition you can imagine, has the kind of ego that invites coaching—even hard coaching. He wants it and knows he needs it. He is a collaborator. His caddie is not hitting the shots for him, but by regarding Greller as a member of the team, Spieth no doubt gets even more out of him. If you listen to Spieth, he often uses the word *we* when talking about a shot he hit, as if Greller had his hands on the club, too. He is not just a caddie, but a partner.

This is one of the lessons I try to get across to every one of my teams. When you share credit, you're not giving something up, you're gaining. If they go from Kentucky and into the NBA, I hope they can surround themselves with people who are not intimidated by their fame or money.

The moment that no one can talk to Jordan Spieth is the moment he begins to decline as a golfer, and perhaps in other ways. But I doubt very much that will occur.

Kenny Payne, one of our assistant coaches, just had a talk with one of our former players that was similar to the interactions between Spieth and his caddie—a sort of keep-it-real reminder. He said to Devin Booker, after his breakout rookie season with the Phoenix Suns: "Beware of everyone telling you how great you are and that they knew it all along. Don't drink that poison. Remember early in the season when we went to your game and you barely played? What got you on the court was your work ethic and your inner drive and that's what you have to remember."

I'm confident that Devin took what Kenny told him to heart. My point is that it's protective to keep truth-tellers in your circle. And it's the job of a leader and mentor—and that's what I consider myself, as does every member of my staff—to stay in that circle and to keep it real.

My current players have me over them right now. If they make it to the NBA, some will be in a position like Spieth's—young and wealthy, with agents and business managers and others who work for them. Some pro players have family members and friends who live with them, a group sometimes referred to as an "entourage." The entourage can be a source of support, but not always. It depends on whether any of those folks are speaking the truth to the player and if he is truly listening.

For as long as they are in my program, I've got a little tighter hold on them. A huge part of my role is to keep it real, to speak honestly and directly to them. In terms of basketball, I might be the first one to have ever done that and made them honestly address the state of their game. I don't want to be the last one, so therefore I have to condition them to be receptive to coaching.

Not everyone wants to coach—truly coach—the extremely

talented. I'm not saying I'm the only one. I'm not. But to coach these kinds of kids, you can't be afraid to tell them the truth. You can't be afraid of hurting their feelings. You can't be afraid that you might mess a kid up. Keeping it real will never harm an athlete, as long as it's done with a caring heart. The way to do harm is to be too timid to challenge them. I recently sent this text message to our players: "I see the talent in you and I am going to rip it out of you no matter how much it will hurt so you can achieve your dreams. It's not going to be easy, but I'm ready for this!"

The Tone Changes. The Message Does Not

I was certainly a little hotter and more quick-tempered when I was a young head coach at UMass. Tony Barbee, a player for me back then and now an assistant coach on my staff at Kentucky, has a pretty good perspective on it. He describes me back then as paying attention to every detail and not letting even the smallest thing go. If my team was running a sprint and they were all supposed to start on the baseline, and I saw one guy with his toe two inches over the line, I'd let them run it but then send them back to start all over. After they ran a second time, if a different guy had his toe over the line, I'd send them back again. I didn't care. We could be there all day.

"He still holds them accountable, but his tone is probably a little bit calmer now most of the time," Tony says. "Generations change, players change, coaches change, and I just think he understands now that you don't have to be at maximum decibel level and maximum intensity every moment of the day to get everything you want out of a player. We knew back then that he had our backs and that he cared about our lives beyond just being basketball players, but I'm not going to lie, it could be rough in that gym at times."

At that stage of my career, I didn't know how to pace myself or delegate like I do now. My assistant coaches and I were at every conditioning session. Every weightlifting session. (The rules were different; we could spend more hours with the team.) Some of my intensity could have been that I was always wired from pushing so hard and not getting enough sleep. In college basketball, it's common to fear that if you lose your first head coaching job, you won't get another. It's not irrational to think that; it happens a lot. A guy gets a job, gets fired after a few years, and never gets another head coaching position.

What makes the challenge even steeper is that most of the jobs available to first-time coaches are at places that have not had any recent success and maybe have no history of winning. It's why you had a chance to get hired at that school—the more established guys have better options. You probably don't have a talented core of returning players to build on. Your facilities aren't likely to be very good, and your recruiting budget is a pittance compared with some of the programs you're trying to beat.

I sometimes ask my kids to play with a sense of desperation. Young coaches—and any leader or CEO in his or her first big job—might sometimes operate with their own kind of desperation. It's also called fear of failure, and it's not a bad thing. But there can be downsides.

At the Hall of Fame weekend, I actually apologized to the guys from my early UMass teams and said I wasn't sure how they survived me. I said it in a light manner, but I meant it. I was a new coach trying to make a name for myself and build a career. My own goals were very much in the foreground—something that changes (or certainly should change) as any leader attains more success. For me, the results of each game probably felt more like life-or-death in the early days.

There was a famous incident back in 1994 when, at a postgame press conference after a hard-fought win over our conference rival, Temple, I very nearly got in a fistfight with their irascible coach, John Chaney. I was a bit cooler-headed than Chaney that night (we would later become friends), but we would have mixed it up if some peacemakers, including a couple of our own players, didn't pull us apart. I don't think I'd let myself be in a scene like that again—or at least I sure hope not.

But anyone who has watched my team on television can see that while I may not run quite as hot, my demands have not lessened one bit. In fact, as the talent level I coach has increased, I am probably more demanding. One difference is that I am probably a little more focused on the development of my individual players rather than wins and losses—though those two things are obviously related.

At halftime, on the way to the locker room, I'll usually stop for one of those quick sideline interviews. We could be leading, 42–18, and the reporter will ask me how we got off to such a big lead. Instead of answering that, I'll tick off three things we didn't do right. One kid threw a careless pass. Another reached for a rebound with one hand instead of grabbing it with two. We didn't get back on defense and gave the other team an easy basket. I'm sure some people laugh. We're up twenty-four points! But that's just how my mind works.

However well we're playing, we can always get better. In addition, I've got to make sure we are not succeeding on physical talent alone—or even on effort. The higher the level you reach, the more important it is to also be technically proficient. I've got players who are easily fooled by their early success and it's important for me to grab them and say, "What you're doing is not going to work when you get up to the next level. It may not work later in the season in the NCAA tournament—or even in the next game."

I may be just a little calmer about it but one of the main points my players have to understand is that success should make them even more self-critical. What can they do to take it up to the next level? That's what world-class athletes do. I told a recent team about Tiger Woods, who when he was dominating the PGA Tour would sometimes irritate competitors by saying after a victory, "Yeah, I won but it wasn't my A-game." People would be like, "But you won by ten strokes!" But he knew he could do better and he was looking for any little thing—in the weight room, in his practice routine, in his nutrition—that could help him do that.

I mentioned Jordan Speith, who might be Tiger's successor. After his historic season, he said he had a number of things he wanted to work on, and when he was asked to be specific, he mentioned "ball-striking." He won all those tourneys and he wasn't striking the ball like he wanted? Apparently not. He wanted to improve.

In the same way, if my players are struggling, I'm usually easier on them, but if they're rolling, I'm usually taking the performance apart and finding anything I can to get them to focus on improvement. After a loss, I'm very brief; after a win, just the opposite.

I asked Fred Smith, the founder and president of FedEx, after we had won the national title in 2012, how he was when things were going well. He said, "That's when I really push and I challenge my senior staff." He said he's never satisfied and demands to know from them "how we're going to improve and get even better." I went on to ask him, "What if it's not going well? What if the roof falls in?" His reply: "I'll always be upbeat in those situations and I smile a lot. I want them to know I have confidence we'll be fine."

I believe the same principle applies to my team and to any business. When things are rocky, people need your reassurance. I don't care how talented they are, people have doubt and anxiety when there's a downturn, for whatever reason, even if it's exterior to the business. They need your reassurance.

JOHN ROBIC ON THE EARLY YEARS

He was tough on those UMass kids. I mean, you've got to think of a fiery, late-twenties to mid-thirties head coach that had a drive to make that place successful and he did that. Has he mellowed? I don't think that's the right word. It's sort of like an athlete who learns to change speeds. He picks up different moves.

A lot of those athletes actually get more intense and more competitive as they get older. But they find different ways to accomplish their goals, and that's how I would describe Cal as he's gotten older. He has more in his arsenal.

The goal has never changed. He's still pushing them. He's still pulling it out of them. But instead of doing it with the undersized or less talented kids we got at UMass, now it's with these five-star prospects, and he's getting them to buy in. It's satisfying because when kids as talented as we're coaching put the work in, the progress can be really fast.

I watched Karl-Anthony Towns on TV the other night. When he got here, he could not sit down in the post. He couldn't hold his position. And here it is a year later and he's doing it in the NBA against grown men. That's a lot of work that he put in, a lot of strength building, a lot of mental resolve. He did that himself, so the credit goes to Karl. But that's the course that Cal set for him. He told him what he had to do and we showed him how. So sitting here and seeing it, it's satisfying.

You Have to Cure Them of Their Delusions

My staff and I often use the word *delusional*. I hope that's not politically incorrect. I'm certainly not talking about the kind of mental delusions that get you put in a psych ward. What we mean is the delusions brought on by two things. One is that the players I coach have experienced a dominating level of success at the youth level of basketball, usually against inferior competition. What this leads to is understandable. When they are matched up against a higher level of competition, first on our own practice court and then in games, they come up against new challenges. Their go-to move, for example, doesn't work in the same way. It's not an automatic basket; the shot gets blocked some of the time. They need to change something, but they don't accept it right away. I restate one of my credos to them: What got you here isn't what's going to get you there (the NBA). Pat Riley says it even better: "My job is to continually define reality."

The other sources of their delusions are parents, family members, and other people who overpraise and enable, leading players to have an exaggerated view of their own capabilities. They love their child and want the best for him but they don't have any real perspective on his capabilities. He's the best player they've ever been around, so the message they send is just keep doing what you're doing. You don't need to change a thing. Just settle in and you'll be as dominant as you were on your high school squad. Their perception can become reality to the family, and you must deal with that.

I know their approach is wrong because I've been through this a few times before. All of these kids are really good, obviously. That's how you get a scholarship offer at an elite basketball program. But they're not supermen. They don't do everything well. But it's common for players to think they do, at least for a while.

I'll have a kid who is, say, an athletic, long-armed perimeter player who I see as a defensive stopper. He's got an okay jump shot that he is still developing and he's a so-so ball handler. I want him to guard one of the other team's best offensive guys and be opportunistic on offense. Cut to the hoop and get some layups and dunks. Crash the boards and get a bucket that way. See if you can make some ten-foot shots. That's the basis of your game until you improve in the other areas.

But when practice starts, and probably even early into the season, there's a pretty good chance he's trying to do stuff that doesn't help him or us. He's dribbling the ball twenty feet from the hoop and jacking up three-point attempts and then looking at me like, "Look, Coach, I've expanded my game." And I have to say, "No, you actually haven't. Not yet. You realize you're not getting anywhere with the ball when you put it on the floor? You're going east and west, and you just dribbled it off your foot and out of bounds. And you're hitting like one out of six of those shots."

I've had players tell me before, "But Coach, you don't know my game," or even, "If you would let me shoot more I would shoot a better percentage."

Players will cling to their delusions even in the face of evidence that should disprove them. It's always a mistake to think they're seeing what you're seeing. And some of those folks from back home are probably still in their ear. "Coach Cal doesn't understand your game! Shooters have to keep on shooting!" The only way to get them to work on their weaknesses—and, as important, to tailor their games to their strengths—is to be very direct and deal with their perceptions.

Here's one example: We're in the middle of the 2014–15 season, we look like a juggernaut—and on most nights, we are. We're ridiculous on defense, one of the best college teams in a generation in that part of the game. Our big guys—Willie Cauley-Stein, Karl-Anthony Towns, Dakari Johnson, and Marcus Lee—form an almost impenetrable wall inside. We have two other players, Trey Lyles and Alex Poythress (before he got hurt), who are the size of power forwards but playing mostly out on the perimeter. Teams can't score near the hoop on us. If they dribble into the lane or pass it inside, the guy with the ball gets lost in a thicket of long arms and massive bodies. He might not even be able to see the basket, let alone get off a shot.

We've beaten Kansas, 72–40, in a game in which they scored just 12 points in the second half. Our defensive performance a month later against UCLA, right before Christmas, was even more dominant. We held them to just 7 points—7—for the whole first half.

But I was not happy with the performance of our frontcourt players on offense. If you really looked at that part of their games, they were actually playing small—like they were six foot five, not seven-footers.

I figured we ought to be able to throw the ball inside and score at will but it was almost the opposite of that. Some games we were getting very little from our post play. Our guards sometimes stopped looking in there because it was unproductive. We were having too many empty trips down the court.

In the spirit of truth-telling, I called the frontcourt players into my office one afternoon to talk about it. I asked them up front, "Can I be real with you? Can I be honest? I'm not trying to hurt anyone's feelings here, but this is what I'm seeing. For every one of you, understand that if you can't score from three feet or get fouled on a college player—and at times a bad college player—do you really think you're ready for the next level? Now, you can't say, 'They never throw me the ball.' But they are throwing you the ball.

Every game that's how we start out. If it stops coming into you, it's only because you're not doing anything good with it."

Karl was one of the players in my office that day. Another was Willie Cauley-Stein, who came to the team as someone who had played more football than basketball. He had been a seven-foot wide receiver at his small high school in Kansas, and on the basketball court there was a big divide between his offensive and defensive abilities (almost like one of those people who take their SATs and their math and English scores look like they came from two different students).

Willie was a defensive genius—long-armed, superfast, and able to guard any position on the floor, including chasing the other team's point guard around if that's what we asked him to do. I've only ever had two other defensive players like him—Marcus Camby and Anthony Davis. But he was behind them both on offense. "Willie, your feet are going to get you in the NBA," I said, by which I meant his ability to move his feet and guard smaller players. "You can leave right now and be fine. But you will never be a significant player unless you can catch it three feet from the basket and either score or get fouled."

Willie's offensive game looked a lot better in practice than in games. He had a jump shot that extended out to about twelve feet. He could put the ball on the floor a little bit and his hands were good enough to have allowed him to catch a bunch of touchdown passes.

Did I want him taking an outside shot with the clock winding down and the game on the line? No, probably not. But I said to him, "Look, take some of those shots. Make yourself a threat or else I'm going to have to take you off the floor at times because we can't be out there playing four-on-five on offense."

I moved from Willie to Dakari Johnson, who was in his second year on the team and a classic center—a big, thick body who had no inclination to play anywhere on offense except planted down low as close to the hoop as he could get. I liked that about him a lot. He was old school, one of the only kids who came to us and asked to be listed on the roster as a center rather than a power forward.

Dakari had worked a lot on his conditioning between his freshman and sophomore seasons, dropping weight and body fat. He could play longer stretches and guard more effectively. He was rebounding the ball and, for a guy his size, doing a good job switching out on pick-and-rolls and stopping guards from penetrating. He wasn't in Willie's class defensively, but he had improved.

But he was still limited offensively, although he had greatly improved his free-throw shooting and his fifteen-foot jump shot. He wasn't explosive off his feet, which is one of the most difficult things to add no matter how hard you go at it in the weight room. But so what? Plenty of guys his size throughout basketball history couldn't jump over a phone book and they still found a way to be effective scorers. It's a matter of making quick, definitive moves and using your body correctly to shield the defender. Dakari wasn't doing that, which is what led to so many of his shots being blocked.

I said to him, "You want me to keep it real, so I'm telling you. If you know about it, you can fix it." And, in fact, by the end of the year, you could see a marked improvement.

- Continually define reality.
- Don't ever assume that your people are seeing things the same way you are. Human beings overestimate their abilities and minimize their failures. That's human nature. It is one of the ways, in fact, that we go forward in life feeling good about ourselves. Happy people do not generally harp on their failings.
- Your role, as someone pledged to "keeping it real," is not to make your people feel bad about themselves. In fact, your critiques should be phrased in the most positive way: Here's how you can improve and be more valuable to the company. And here is what's in it for you in terms of job satisfaction, advancement, and compensation. That doesn't mean demanding any less.
- No one under you should ever feel they have reached a plateau, even if they are in a mature phase of their career. Your role is to keep putting goals and rewards in front of people. It is the *only* way a company moves forward—on the backs of its energized, ambitious workforce. Never make the mistake of thinking that by making people uncomfortable— meaning you want more from them—you are making them unhappy. They should feel complimented that you believe they can grow.
- When you do criticize, if your people know you care about them— truly care about their lives, their families, and their concerns separate and apart from the workplace—they will not resent the criticism or take it negatively. They will accept it and act upon it.

Keep It Real, but Don't Be Intimidating

Coaching, like any form of leadership, is not so much knowledge based as it is wisdom based. You acquire it over the years and build on it. If you're lucky, you survive your youthful errors. One of the things that excited me most about doing this book is the opportunity to truly look inward and explore my own methods. What have I done that works? What have I tossed out over the years because it was not effective? What should I discard because it's not working and I don't even realize it? More broadly, what can be taken from my methods—and the highly collaborative sport I coach—and applied to the business world?

I have to set certain standards for my players, hold them accountable, and have consequences. But I don't want them to be afraid of me. In my own mind, I think, Why would they be? They're making me way bigger than I am. But my staff will sometimes say to me, "Cal, they see you as intimidating," and I'm like, "What? What are you talking about?"

I don't see myself that way. Any players can walk right into my office, and they frequently do. The team is at my house all the time. I'm Italian, in case you didn't know, so I hug them. I kiss them on the head. We've got a rule on our team that you can't end any interaction without touching. You give a fist bump, a hug, or whatever but it's got to be something. My players are family, and I do think that, on a human level, they regard me in the same way.

But it's what I represent that can be intimidating. They believe that I control their playing time and, to a certain extent, their futures. They come to Lexington—for a year or for however long—and I am the person they think they have to please in order to realize their dreams. They've got to get through me.

I see it as much more in their control—based on how dedicated they are to the grind, on their performances in practices and games—but I have to accept the reality of what my coaches tell me. My assistant coaches often serve as a sort of bridge. If a player needs help interpreting me, figuring out what I mean, the assistants are there as a sounding board. Am I really down on a kid when I yell at him in practice? (No.) Do I hold grudges? (No.) If a kid has a bad stretch, will I give up on him? (No.) I could tell them all that but I understand that sometimes it's a role that falls to my assistants.

Fear, of a certain kind, does have its uses. It's not good if you have a fear of missing a last-second shot, because then you won't take the shot. You'll shirk the responsibility and give it to a team-mate. But a more broad-based fear of failure—"I'm going to work as hard as I can because I'm afraid if I don't I'll squander this opportunity"—that's different. The one who feels that way takes the shot. He wants the opportunity to show who he is. Even if he misses it, he'll shoot it again the next time. I'll take that kid every time.

The reality that some players may see me as a source of fear is one of the biggest challenges of my job. It's a place where my own success probably does not help me. The better we do, the bigger that incoming player may perceive me. I'm sure it's a challenge for a great many people in leadership positions. You're in the corner office. You've got the big desk, the window with the big view. Your trophies and trinkets are all over your office. It makes you feel good but maybe it has the opposite effect on someone else.

You can say, "Hey, let's go sit on the couch and talk," but the degree of ease that person feels—and how he perceives you—is not entirely under your control. It never is.

I use the word *empowerment* a lot with my team. I want them individually empowered—feeling in control of their own futures—and empowered as a group. That should take the onus off me. I don't loom as large if they're in control. But that's a challenge each year, with each new set of kids.

You Must Give Recognition (and Also Be Ready to Take Responsibility)

There's no getting around the fact that a big part of coaching involves correcting. You blow the whistle and tell your team to run the play again, this time the right way. You level with a player and explain what he's got to fix in order to earn time on the court. You don't want to hurt his feelings, but if you sugarcoat it, you're doing him no favors.

The stuff we do is not for the tenderhearted. If you have that kind of constitution, maybe you should go into the fine arts— piano or violin, whatever, though I hear those instructors can be pretty brutal, too. The sad fact is that if you want to perform at the highest level, if you want to achieve anything in life, you'd better be able to stand up to criticism. What's the venue in which all you hear are congratulations for how wonderful you are, and that propels you to a lifetime of high achievement? There isn't one. It would ruin you. It's my role as a leader to take responsibility when we don't play well. I will never blame a player. When we play well and we win, I give the players all the credit.

In 2008, my Memphis team had a nine-point lead with 2:40 to go in the national championship game against Kansas. We were the worst free-throw shooting team in the NCAA Tournament and everyone knew that was our Achilles' heel. We proceeded to miss five of six free throws. Kansas made some ridiculous shots, pushed the game to overtime, and because we were shorthanded in overtime with foul trouble, we ended up losing the game. When the game ended I had one comment: "This was on me. When you have a nine-point lead with 2:40 to go, you should win the game. The coach should win the game." I didn't want any players being scarred the rest of their lives as though they lost the national championship game. I took that on myself.

Now, I will critique a player's performance. I might say, "He can't play that way if he wants to stay in the lineup." Sometimes if the press asks about a kid's poor performance, I'll say that I have no idea—go ask him. And then I'll make sure that the player is among those designated to talk to the press, so he has to come out to the podium and answer. It's good for them. My thinking is that you should own your great games, and your bad ones, too. But if we lose, that's on me. And if we win, the kids get all the credit.

In the old days, younger college players were sometimes protected from the press by some coaches. "He's just a freshman; you can't talk to him." I don't think that's a good idea now. Maybe you're still just eighteen years old, but if you're thinking you are going to step into pro ball in the next year or two, you have to know that they let the press right into the locker room in the NBA. In New York, Los Angeles, Chicago, or Boston, there will be twenty-five of them in a semicircle around your dressing cubicle, pointing their cameras and microphones at you, wanting to know what caused you to throw the ball out of bounds with the clock ticking down in a tie game.

Did you think you saw an open teammate? Lose the handle on it? Mistake the referee for one of your own guys? Maybe you just panicked. Is that what you did? You'd better have an answer, and I figure it's a good idea to let my players practice giving them. Where they plan on going, they will be held accountable.

But an equally important part of "keeping it real" is giving praise, which I try my best to do at every teaching opportunity. It's the other side of the coin. You can't just beat on people. If that's all you do, you're not a leader—you're a bully. You're engaging in what I call "destructive criticism."

Going back to my UMass days, I always tried to focus on giving praise or "catching" someone at doing something right. We had a player, Harper Williams, whom I nicknamed "the warrior." He always had energy in the tank and I'd point it out to the rest of the kids. When others practiced like he did, I'd single them out as well.

And I firmly believe that it should be specific praise because that always counts for more. Let me start by first giving an example as it relates to my coaching staff. John Robic prepares the scouting reports of the opposing team. Let's say that he has identified something that the other team is likely to do to try to defend one of our typical offensive sets. He suggests a tweak we can use to counter it, and it leads to easy buckets for us and makes the difference between a win and a loss. Afterward, rather than just saying, "Great job, Robes" (his nickname), it's a lot better if I reference exactly what he did and how much he contributed to our success. Specific praise counts for more because it shows that you thought deeply about a person's contributions. Even after thirty years of coaching, I need to do a better job searching out good things to praise people for.

Maybe what I just wrote seems obvious. Why wouldn't you praise someone? But the fact is that people in charge of big, fast-moving enterprises aren't always very good at it, or they don't do it enough. If you doubt that, just go out and ask a bunch of people if their boss appreciates them.

Sometimes it's too easy when you're the person in charge to think, Hey, I put this person on my staff and pay them a good salary, so they must know how much I appreciate what they do. But it doesn't work that way, especially when you're asking for an extraordinary effort and the kind of long hours that can take someone away from their family. (To those in the business world, I'd also add: Praise doesn't cost you anything, so why wouldn't you give it?)

The same principles apply to the issue of giving proper recognition to my players, though it's a little more complicated. Coaching athletes, and particularly extremely talented ones engaged in elite-level competition, is a particular thing. You're asking them to push through physical discomfort, if not pain. They're up against opponents engaged in the same struggle. The difference between a win and a loss is one not just of extreme effort but also, at crucial moments, of the ability to play mistake-free.

As a coach, you can easily fall into a warrior mentality where it's all push, push, push. Recognizing what someone did right—as opposed to pointing out their errors—might seem alien to that culture. You fall into the trap of thinking that if you pat someone on the back, they'll become satisfied and complacent. But that kind of thinking is not appropriate or productive.

Our players aren't computers. You can't plug them in and figure they'll just keep on clicking along, mistake-free. You want them to dive on the floor after every loose ball, but some days they don't have as much fuel in the tank. On balance, the good stuff they do just has to outweigh the bad.

I've found over the years that even my most talented players need affirmation. Even if I think otherwise and they seem fully confident, I'm wrong. They need to hear from me that I notice what they're doing right. I'll stop a practice at any time and point to a kid and say, "Did you see that?! Did everyone see what he just did?!"

It's usually after a player has been struggling with something and I've been on him. Say, for example, we've been trying to get him to just catch the ball on the offensive end and pause for a beat—so he can rise up and shoot, or square up and drive. But every time he touches the ball, the first thing he does is bounce it. It's a common mistake, and it completely robs an offensive player of his options. This player finally does it right on the practice court and I make a big deal of it. I'll stop everyone and say, "Did you see that?" We celebrate. Or it's a player who keeps reaching for rebounds with one hand instead of reaching and grabbing with two. Boom! We stop again because I need to affirm it.

I do this to let the player know I noticed that he did what I asked. But it's also a teaching technique. I want him to think about how that felt in his body when he did it correctly. He can't replicate it unless it's in his muscle memory.

If you want a certain behavior, you must reward that behavior in real time and in evaluations. In our case, real time means that when it happens in a practice or game, we immediately recognize it in a positive way, which reinforces that behavior. I will stop practice when I see a player playing and reacting to situations in ways that make that player the best version of himself. I may not stop a game, but I'll also give positive affirmation during a game in real time, followed up by doing it in timeouts, at halftime, and postgame. I won't even acknowledge a behavior, even if it has a positive result, if the action does not fit the vision we have and what we're looking for.

Like all basketball teams, we watch tape of our games, usually before practice, in an amphitheater down the hall from the gym. It's got theater seating and plenty of leg room for our very tall athletes. I'm dealing with young guys and short attention spans. We keep the film sessions short, usually about ten minutes or less.

One thing I do is vary the tone. I'm tough. I'm supportive. And quite a bit of the time, I try to be funny. You hear sometimes that a team has "stopped listening" to a coach or tuned him out. That can happen at the pro level when you have the same players over the course of many years. But even on the college level, it's a long season. The predominant voice on the practice floor and in the film room is mine, and I don't want it to sound the same way all the time. I think that's important for any leader. Change it up when you can. The same somber or angry or insistent tone, day after day, is deadening. Sometimes you've got to entertain them.

I never want to embarrass one of my players. As I said, a big thing that I preach is the willingness to fight—not in throwing punches, obviously, but to sustain effort. So we'll watch film of one of our players grabbing a rebound with two hands, which is what we want. "Great!" I'll say. I'll advance the film; we'll watch him try to secure the ball, and then we see he gets it punched out of his hands. From there he gets pushed aside and lands in the laps of the cheerleaders.

"Wait a second," I'll say. "How did he get there?" Everybody laughs, but the point is made. Not tough enough. No fight. I'm big on visual evidence. Just as I want them to see what they look like at their best, I show them the opposite.

We want to play with ferocity, so that's how we practice. It doesn't matter what day it is or what time of the season—we could be coming up on a national championship game. I want guys dunking the ball in practice, not just politely laying it in. I don't care if it's a drill we're doing without defense, a three-on-three half-court exercise, or a full-court scrimmage, dunk it. If they do it like they're trying to rip the rim from the backboard, all the better.

What we do is not life or death—it's just basketball—but I'd say the same about most businesses. There's virtually no workplace where a little humor does not improve the atmosphere and ultimately the performance. (Even in the life-and-death ones like the military or the most challenging hospital settings, the fact is that humor and levity are basic human needs.)

We give an award called the helmet award. When a player dunks on somebody during practice, he gets to put a Kentucky football helmet on the player he dunked on, the so-called dunkee. We know that, after practice, we're going to put the helmet on him and take a picture of both him and the person he dunked on, and that will go up on the locker room wall. Those pictures will stay there until someone else gets dunked on. We have an absolute blast with it.

BEYOND THE ARC

- As a leader, take responsibility when things go poorly. You can still critique and evaluate, but you don't want your employees afraid of failure.
- Keeping it real doesn't mean keeping it negative. It is equally important to catch your people doing good things and hold them—and their actions—up as a model.
- Celebrating success is related, in a way, to muscle memory. You must take a step back, regard what you've done, and remember it in order to be able to replicate it. If you let the moment pass, you have wasted a teaching opportunity.
- Don't forget humor. It's welcome (and needed) in any workplace.
- What has just been celebrated becomes an expectation. You did it once—made the big sale; became more efficient; solved the bug in the software—and so you ought to be able to do it again and again.
- Praise is cheap and you have an inexhaustible supply of it. There's no excuse for not giving it. But the people you lead cannot depend on your affirmation for their self-esteem.
- Understand the difference between good fear and bad fear. Fear of missing a game-winning shot is bad fear—it causes a player to hesitate to step up in a big situation and take the shot. A broader-based fear of failure—the anxiety of coming up short of expectations—is good. It causes a person to work harder.
- Very important point: You—the CEO, the boss, the coach—do not want to be a source of fear or intimidation. You want to inspire people, not terrorize them. If you've had success, you may be intimidating to those under you, through no fault of your own, but you should be aware of it and do what you can to mitigate it.
- Use your closest managers under you as a sounding board to let you know how the "troops" are regarding you. They will know better than you can ascertain for yourself, and you have to demand that they tell you the truth, that they keep it real with you.

Tailor the Message to the Individual

A lot of the things I'm thinking about as I write these chapters come down to the difference between being a modern-day leader and being one whose approach is rooted in the past. I'm not sure that my coaches, back when I was growing up, spent a great deal of time thinking about the individual learning styles of their players. That just wasn't the philosophy at the time. Sports teams were almost like military units, and there were positive aspects to that. Everything was fair, equitable, understood. You fell in with the program and learned not to expect too much special handling.

But I'm sure some kids got left behind. I would not have been aware of it at the time, but knowing what I know now, I realize it had to be the case. If you couldn't fit yourself into the mold you probably weren't going to make it. I studied marketing in college, not psychology, but everyone now is more psychologically attuned. Teachers, bosses, parents, and, yes, coaches. It is an expectation now that you will regard those under you as individuals and—within the bounds of being fair to everyone—try to give them what they need to thrive.

Several years into my tenure at UMass, I was coaching a young man whom I didn't yet know well. If I really went hard at him, he would just shut down. Once, he just walked off the court. I was doing it wrong. It was not the way to coach that kid. I came to understand that his upbringing had been really hard. In various ways, he had been beaten down, and shutting down was his defense mechanism. I changed my approach to him, as well I should have.

I'm not in the business of "saving" kids. Very occasionally, I've had a player where it just wasn't working and my own circle of advisers told me that I was getting as much out of the player as was possible and just had to lower my expectations. In one such case, I remember Bruiser Flint, an assistant for me at UMass who went on to his own coaching career, saying to me about one kid, "Cal, you're not Father Flanagan. You've done everything you can. You just have to let it go."

Believe me, I'm tough because I'm in a tough business. Soft players do not survive at our level of college basketball, let alone in the NBA, so I have to prepare them for that. Ask any of my players if I was easy on them, and you won't find one who will say yes.

But I'm not in the business of just standing by as people struggle and fall through the cracks. I recruit extreme talent. Just like in any business, extreme talent does not always equate with a person who is settled, secure, and able to deal easily with all the pressures and expectations falling on him. All that is accentuated because I'm dealing with young people. They're figuring out not just how to make it as basketball players but also who they are as human beings. It's up to me to peel back the onion, get down into the layers of their personality, and determine what I've got to touch to pull the best out of them.

When I meet a young man and his family for the first time, I ask them this: What is your story? Tell me about the history of your family. Just because a player is big and looks like a grown man doesn't mean he is. In most cases, mine are not. I have meetings with my players to get to know them even better, to understand what they are feeling and see how I can help them reach their full potential. Each of them is different. They need to be treated fairly but that doesn't mean I treat them all the same.

If you are a CEO—or the leader of a smaller team of talented, creative individuals—you need to capture what each person has to offer and build whatever support they need under them to keep on going. Otherwise, you're wasting a human resource.

It's not like you're giving something up if you take that approach. Just the opposite. You're helping your team move forward. And not to be too preachy about it, but especially when you're dealing with a young person, I think it's your moral obligation. Why would you let that person fail? You think you can get someone just as good, but easier to deal with? That may be your choice, but it's not the way I want to operate.

As I said in the introduction, to lead extreme talent often means taking on complicated individuals. Depending on the day, they're high-strung, stubborn, egotistical—overconfident or insecure—tough on the outside but easily wounded. That's the challenge we have in leading and bringing out the best in people.

Every player is different in terms of the affirmation they need. Eric Bledsoe was a top high school player in Birmingham, Alabama, and part of my first recruiting class at Kentucky, in the same group with John Wall and DeMarcus Cousins. He was good—really good—but he didn't have quite the reputation of those other two. On top of that, he did not have the same bulletproof ego.

John Wall didn't need me to give him a lot of recognition. He knew who he was. His primary physical gift—unbelievable speed that allowed him to just blow by people on the dribble—was no less a weapon when he stepped up from high school to the college level. There still weren't too many guys who could keep up with him and he knew it.

DeMarcus, or Boogie as many called him, was a massive human being with soft hands, a good shooting touch, and quick feet. He couldn't be guarded at the college level. He still can't be guarded in the NBA. He is a free spirit, an entertainer, and an athlete with a motor that sometimes sputters on and off, depending on his mood. The only force that can stop Boogie is himself. He didn't need much recognition from me, either, and usually required the opposite—I had to be direct and firm with him.

Back when I was recruiting DeMarcus, I knew he was not

choosing a program without his mother's approval. Afterward, when I asked her why she sent him to me, she said, "Because he respected you as a coach, and I knew you were not not afraid of him."

DeMarcus and John were really special as players, and Eric was letting himself be overwhelmed by them. He was too eager to defer, and my role was to keep reminding him that he, too, had extreme talent. If his talent was not at the level of the other two, it was just a tick below—but he didn't feel that way.

A complicating factor was that John and Eric both came in as point guards, which was considered unusual. Most teams line up with a designated point guard, the guy who is supposed to run the show alongside a shooting guard who will, in theory, take more of the scoring burden. But it doesn't have to be so strictly defined. If you have guards with a combination of those skills, they can share the positions—one can take the burden off the other—and that was my plan with Eric and John.

When I was recruiting them, some people told Eric not to come with us because he wouldn't play much, or he would never be in his natural position. I knew that wasn't true and told him so. If John played the point guard exclusively, defenses might crawl all over him and take away from his scoring. Eric, on the other hand, might have been overwhelmed if he had to run the point for thirty minutes a game as a freshman. I was thinking about the start of the season (it's a lot to ask of a freshman still getting acclimated, especially on a team expected to contend for a national title) as well as tournament time, when the pressure would really increase.

I figured they could work it out organically, within the flow of the game. One would end up with the ball in his hands; the other would run to the wing and look for opportunities within our "dribble-drive" offense—a free-flowing attack that takes advantage of the skills and improvisation of all five players on the court. What I envisioned was really the ultimate collaboration between two very talented players; they would each give a little something up but gain a lot more in return, as would our team.

It worked, most of the time, but I still could see that Eric was considering himself the junior partner, and I didn't want that. It was based more on his personality than his skills. He was very strong for his stature and really quick. When he had his confidence, he was completely fearless. He could do stuff that was out of the norm.

I became his cheerleader. I took him aside a couple of times and said, "I see you trying to blend into the background at times. Just stop it! You're too good. Create your own space for shots. Create space so you can make plays for others. If you keep stepping back, you're not doing yourself any good and you're not helping the team as much as you can."

In team meetings I made Eric speak up. I made him become involved in the scouting reports. I made him see how much confidence I had in him as a player and a leader. In any enterprise, you know that your best people are not always your most assertive people. You have to bring it out of them, or else you won't get their full talent.

There are certain moments in the course of the season that are turning points for teams and for individual players, too. Eric's was a mid-January game against Florida in Gainesville, a tough opponent in a hostile environment. Their coach at the time, Billy Donovan, is one of the best defensive tacticians in the business, and he was determined to shut down John and put the pressure on Eric to carry the load. It was a good strategy but probably one of the best things that could have happened for us, because Eric accepted the challenge.

He scored 25 points on 10-of-13 shooting—including three of four from beyond the three-point arc—and added 7 rebounds and

5 assists. It was a monster game, and afterward, there was no way he didn't realize how good he was.

One of the stories after the game said, "Attention, Southeastern Conference. Kentucky has a freshman point guard capable of beating teams in a variety of ways. And it's not John Wall." I couldn't have written it better myself! That was exactly what I envisioned when I put them together. I was able to say to Eric after the Florida game, "This is the best version of you. You need to own it and know that's how you should be every time you take the floor." I didn't mean that he should score 25 points in every game, but there was no reason he could not carry that swagger into each one.

The naysayers had tried to tell them they would subtract from each other but I believed it would be just the opposite. In business, you'd call it synergy. Playing them together had a multiplier effect: Each of them developed non–point guard skills that otherwise they might not have used, and each became a better point guard by seeing what it was like to play off the ball.

For a long time, Eric didn't believe the NBA would be interested in him. He didn't come out of high school as a kid who it was assumed would go quickly into the league. I'd have to say to him, "Eric, are you kidding? Do you have any idea how good you are?" John Wall and his other teammates would say the same, and in fact, one key to Eric's growth was that John was constantly in his ear, letting him know how good he was. He became one of Eric's biggest fans and supporters. Playing two point guards together was not something I had done before, or that was common elsewhere, and it wouldn't have worked without John's affirmation of his teammate. He was secure enough within himself to be a true servant leader and lift up his teammate.

Eric got drafted at the end of the season, the No. 18 pick, by the Oklahoma City Thunder—which I don't think would have happened if he had not been paired with John Wall. (And I'm not sure John would have been the first overall pick without Eric.) He now plays for the Phoenix Suns, where last season he averaged 20 points and 6 assists a game, which are big numbers. He is on his way to being an NBA all-star and would have made it already if not for some injuries.

Don't Be Afraid of Pushback

I refer to each season and my entire relationship with a player—whether it lasts one season or four—as a tug-of-war. And the reason is that I'm dealing with very strong-willed people. You have to understand that they have already experienced success—in fact, they've been dominant—doing things their way. And then they get to me and I say, "Look, this thing you've been doing all your life, it won't work up here. You've just got to believe me." Why is it surprising that they wouldn't excel right away, and push back on what I want them to do? It's not.

Maybe a big kid has a spin move in the lane that just killed everybody every time he did it in high school. He bounced the ball, lowered his butt, made the big spin, and powered to the hoop for a dunk. Unstoppable. He could score 30 points anytime he wanted. If he was really feeling his oats, he'd go for 40.

That was Julius Randle's go-to move. I had to say, "Look, Julius, a defender is going to be waiting for you at the back end of that spin. He's going to have his feet planted and you're going to bowl him over and get called for a charge. Or how about this? Some little guard is going to crack down and slap the ball away in the middle of that spin and now instead of you dunking the ball, the other team is headed in the other direction and they've got a dunk."

Julius, at six foot nine and 250 pounds, was used to just flicking off smaller players like they were gnats. I tried to tell him: The ones you're going to compete against up here are older, smarter, and a lot stronger. Some of them are twenty-two years old. They're not intimidated by you. Show them the ball and they'll rip it right out of your hands.

When I say I want pushback, I'm not referring to kids talking back or showing disrespect. But you don't want them to just roll over, and Julius didn't. An elite athlete has an edge, a thing inside him that believes that he can impose his will by doing things his way—the same way he's been doing it all his life. When it stops working, the first thing he does is double down. He tries to do that same thing, just only a little better. I'll spin faster! Instead of charging into the guy, I'll spin back in the other direction . . . a double spin!

Julius had a fantastic season for us, averaging a double-double—15 points and 10 rebounds. His work ethic and will to win were at a high level, as any fan could see because the kid was drenched in sweat from just about the opening tip-off. He didn't wander off to the perimeter; he planted himself down low and banged. He was one of the biggest reasons we got all the way to the 2014 national championship game, but believe me, we did have a tug-of-war.

In an early-season loss to Michigan State, he had 27 points and 13 rebounds, an unbelievable performance for a player in his third college game—unless you also take into account that he had 8 turnovers. Eight. That's a number that not even your point guard, who has the ball in his hands much of the time, should ever approach.

I don't treat my players tenderly. Maybe if I had them for four years, I would go about it a little differently, but these are guys who expect to be in the NBA in a year, where they'll be held accountable. Nobody cares about their feelings. Your contract is based on performance. If you've got problems in your game that you don't fix, you'll be out of the league in a hurry. (Every teenager the NBA drafts takes somebody's roster spot—and sometimes it's the spot of a guy who was drafted a few years earlier, when he was a teenager. When you get up there, you'd better be ready or you could be gone before you know it.)

Whatever critique I give in the locker room is generally the same thing I'll tell the media. If that puts more pressure on players to change, so be it. As I said before, I will take responsibility for the loss, but each player has to take responsibility for his performance. I told the writers after the Michigan State loss, "Julius had eight turnovers for one reason: He held the ball. He tried to go against five guys. You can't play basketball that way. The ball moves and then you attack."

Seven times in our first sixteen games, Julius had at least four turnovers. He kept doing the things that I asked him to stop. It was his way of pushing back, not out of disrespect, as I said—but because he had that edge about him, the confidence that if he just did that same thing, but better, it would work. From my end, I kept pulling on the rope.

I kept telling him: Make quick, definitive moves to the basket. Get the basketball past the defender. Don't be a "ball-stopper"— someone who makes two, three, four different feints before trying to get a shot. If it's not there for you, just pass the ball back out. He finally got it. In the homestretch of our season, our last fourteen games, Julius had just one game in which he had as many as four turnovers. He had bought in and "surrendered" to what we were telling him—but first he had to find out that his way wouldn't work. That's just how I view it. I'm in a season-long battle. My will against their will. It's not unpleasant at all; it's just coaching.

In the second game of the NCAA tournament, we were matched

up against the No. 1 seed, Wichita State, who came into the game at 35-0. We had 10 losses but were coming on strong mainly because I had finally gotten the upper hand in my individual tugs-of-war with several of our players. The seeding was unfair to Wichita State; we were too good a team for them to have to play in the first weekend.

In what was a truly great college basketball game, up and down, with big shots being hit on both sides, we beat them, 78–76. Julius put up his usual double-double—13 points and 10 rebounds.

If you looked more deeply into the box score, he had six assists—a big number for a power forward—against just one turnover. Every time Wichita State sent two defenders at him, he quickly moved the ball to an open teammate. It was a mind-set, a skill set, and an example of court awareness that he absolutely had not been capable of at the start of the season.

People who are critics of the current system say, "What can you really get done in five months?" Well, we got that done.

Julius was fortunate enough to be a lottery pick of the Los Angeles Lakers, a team that needed him badly and a team that he badly wanted to play for. Unfortunately, he suffered a season-ending injury in the first game of his rookie season. He recovered and began again in 2016, had a great season, and is on his way to being the all-star I think he can become.

BEYOND THE ARC

- Treating everyone fairly doesn't mean treating everyone the same. Past performance and personality will lead you to deal with people on an individual basis. You can be firm, but being fair isn't the same for everyone.
- Strong-willed people can seem more difficult to lead. Ultimately, they are usually worth it. Their will is what drives them forward, and once you get it turned in the right direction, their potential is unleashed.
- Some of your most strong-willed players will really challenge you. You can never let go of the rope, and you can't be afraid to lead. Use their strengths and will to challenge them even harder.
- Understand that in some cases, your best people are not always your most assertive people. Sometimes you have to coach aggressiveness, just like you would any other skill.
- Use a mix of team meetings and individual meetings to make your points. Your office is your sanctum. Use it when you need to make quiet but firm points with an individual, and then reemphasize your expectations for individuals in a group setting. Everyone in the group should know what the expectations are for each individual so they can hold each other accountable.

5

THE METRICS DON'T LIE

The great ones in any line of work are always competing against themselves. I use metrics to give my players additional ways to truly measure themselves and as a means of making competitive people even more competitive. How can they achieve continuous improvement? How can they become more efficient? How can I educate them on which of their actions on the basketball court amount to what I call "winning plays"?

We have one essential metric in basketball that will never change: wins and losses. It's what we're judged on and what we should be judged on. But there are many components that go into those wins and losses that can be broken out and measured—both team and individual statistics. If we use them correctly, they can drive our performance to a higher level.

My emotional connection with players is always going to count more than any columns of numbers that get put in front of me, so I never want to go too crazy with statistics. But I'm also aware that we are living in an increasingly data-driven world and I'd be foolish not to take full advantage of every metric available to me and the analysis that comes with them.

I use metrics in several different ways. One is to help make a point with an individual player, and sometimes those numbers do not have to be very advanced. They can just be the old-fashioned stats that come out of a box score. (There's a lesson here: Don't get so lost in the new whiz-bang numbers available to you that you forget that the traditional ones can also effectively tell a story.)

To give one example, I talk sometimes about guys being "play starters" or "play finishers." Basically, the play starter is a player with the ball in his hands a lot. He can get his own shot on the perimeter—or drive to the hoop—or penetrate and dish to an open teammate. He has to have a good handle on the ball and be a sound decision maker. The finisher is the player on the other end of the equation. He's going to take one or two dribbles, at most, and shoot—or maybe just dunk it at the end of an alley-oop pass. I don't want this guy with the ball in his hands twenty feet from the hoop; if he ends up with it out there, he needs to quickly give it up.

Sometimes, I've got play finishers who think they are initiators and I can just show them some old-school stats—assists and turnovers—to make them see the real story. I had one kid who was like, "Coach, but you don't get it, I really think I'm a good passer." And I said, "No, let's look at the statistics. On the season so far, you've got twenty turnovers and just four assists. So you can pass. You just don't pass them to our team."

Keep Score Every Day

People trust what they can see on a spreadsheet. The more data the better—and I'm good with that as long as it doesn't drown out your own powers of observation and intuition. But what you think you're seeing can occasionally fool you. What you get from the numbers helps fill in a complete picture.

Companies have long looked at their quarterly earnings, but advanced computing has allowed them to go much deeper and more easily track their own behaviors in real time—as well as the likes, dislikes, and habits of their customers.

Any person in a position of responsibility should want access to as much statistical information as possible. (What's the alternative? "Nah, I don't want to see that stuff; I'll just trust my gut.") The medical care that we receive is now partly based on the use of "big data"—number crunching of the outcomes for large numbers of treatments for various conditions. In the coming years, they'll increasingly put our individual genetics into the mix.

Political campaigns use advanced metrics and target voters based on their habits and characteristics. Where do you shop? What kind of car do you drive? Are you married or single and how often do you attend a house of worship? They run all that stuff through a program and get a pretty good idea of how you're likely to vote—or what powers of persuasion they can use to try to get you to vote a different way.

More and more, people are tracking their own metrics in their normal, day-to-day lives. You see your friends walking around with Fitbits and other devices that count the steps they take. They're using devices to measure their heart rates and sleep patterns. You can even plug the types of foods you eat and calories you consume into a computer and a program will tell you how to make modifications to lose weight.

In business—as in basketball—one thing that metrics can help you with is the normal human emotion to let yourself feel too good or too comfortable about something that, upon closer examination, is not such a great thing. For example, let's say you've attracted more customers. What was the cost of getting them? Did you really measure everything or did you just look at the stuff that weighs in your favor? The corporate world has always wanted to know this, but now you can do it on a more granular level.

It's just a short hop from metrics to accountability. In Wal-Mart's corporate headquarters in Bentonville, Arkansas, there's a big sign that says: TODAY'S STOCK PRICE IS X, TOMORROW'S IS UP TO YOU. When you know the numbers, you should feel required to have an impact on them.

My good friend John Schnatter, founder and CEO of Papa John's Pizza, is someone who is on top of his business and its trends. He is on top of every metric. He knows everything from the cost of cheese per pizza, to the return he gets from advertisement, to shipping costs, to you name it. All this has helped him become an industry leader who continues to grow his business. David Novak, the former chairman of Yum! Brands (Taco Bell, KFC, Pizza Hut, and other restaurant chains) is also a man I know and respect. He says that businesses have to "take stock every day." I'm sure he knows more now about his own company's spending and the habits of his consumers than he ever has before—probably down to what day of the week and what hour of the day a person is most likely to order a pepperoni pizza as opposed to extra cheese.

My version of taking stock every day is that we keep score every day. A person walking into one of our practices—or the practices of just about any professional or major college basketball team—might be surprised to see that the scoreboard is almost always on and the clock is running. Everything we do in a Kentucky basketball practice is timed. It's measured in various ways. We compete. Even in drills, we're not just going through the motions—we're usually trying to win at something. The points go up on the scoreboard. We log the winners and losers and it all gets compiled and analyzed. (If you look at the word *accountable*, you see that the root of it is *count*. Well, we count everything.)

The statistics give us information but they also serve as motivation and drive us to practice harder. Any elite sports training has to be based on competition. Michael Phelps, the Olympic swimmer, was famous for his intense practice sessions, especially when he was younger and his body could stand up to it. His coach, Bob Bowman, set a target time for everything within a practice that Phelps swam, and the goal was always really fast—more so than for other elite swimmers, who sometimes trained at a more leisurely rate just to build up their aerobic capacity. Bowman believed that since he didn't want Phelps to swim slowly in meets, why would he ever practice swimming slowly? Phelps built up his endurance, but it was with times that Bowman set that no other swimmer would ever think of trying to hit.

When we go hard, simulating game conditions—or, at times, even going beyond them in terms of our physical output—the numbers I get from practice are really good. I accept some injury risk, because there is always a possibility of that when you go full tilt. I'm less worried about fatigue. My players are young; they can take it. Toward the end of the season, I'll pull back some so they don't go into games with heavy legs. But if we did it a different way and we coasted through practices, trying to conserve energy or lessen risk, all I would learn is who's good at playing with 75 percent effort.

We track our shots in practice: in five-on-five scrimmages, three-on-three, and half-court sets, and when we stop the action to practice from the foul line. We've got it on videotape and there's also somebody sitting in a little viewing area above the court, logging stats. It gives a big sample size and a more accurate sense of a player's true shooting ability than if we just looked at shots taken in games. But the practice shots must be taken under duress, like they are in a game, and when a player is winded or even fatigued from competition. (It's a lot easier to shoot when you're rested.)

Our statistics have grown beyond traditional basketball numbers and now include biometrics and other measurements based on the monitors our players wear during practice. We track, for instance, their heart rates, which we can measure against their known baselines. They also wear GPS devices so I know how much ground they cover during a practice and how many "bursts"—a measurement of the speed of their first three steps—they have while they're on the floor.

The data is fairly consistent over the course of a season. Certain players just move more and log more distance. Jamal Murray was one who was almost always at or near the top of the chart. We ran him around a lot of screens in our offense, from side to side on the baseline and then popping out beyond the three-point arc, so that was a lot of steps. And he was just, by his nature, energetic and active. He didn't stop. Trey Lyles, who played for me in 2014–15, was a much bigger guy but similar to Jamal—very focused, and a hard practicer. He covered a lot of ground in practice. These types of guys are very talented, but they're also self-made, and the data bears that out.

The way I use this information is a great example of using metrics as a communication tool. I've been at this long enough that I can see when one of my players is lagging. I might notice a kid fading and wonder, Is he sick? Is something else going on—an injury he doesn't want to tell me about, a problem with a teammate, something academic, bad news from home? He might say, "No, Coach, I'm fine. I haven't been letting up." But I can show him these numbers and say, "This stuff doesn't lie. You're not yourself."

At that point, I've got a better chance of finding out what's going on. Lots of times, he isn't feeling well or he's got a minor injury and I can say, "You've got to get that checked out. You can't let it linger or it could get worse."

BEYOND THE ARC

- Use metrics to confirm your own powers of observation. Do they bear out what you are seeing in the performance of your company and your people and do they match what you intuitively believe to be true? Or are they telling a different story?
- Decide which numbers really matter to you. Break it down to a manageable set of them. You don't want to get so buried in metrics that you become a less effective leader and motivator.

The Best "System" Is the One That Works

I don't have an offensive and defensive system that I install year after year at Kentucky, and then just plug my players in and teach them to run it. That's not how we do things. What we run is tailored to the components of my roster. I'm going to do what's best for my players, not what I'm most comfortable with or what makes me feel good about myself.

Do I have an ego and think I'm a good coach? Of course I do. I don't think I could be successful if I felt otherwise. But there's nothing we do on the court that I invented or trademarked and thus has to be the signature way we play. Like just about every basketball coach, other than a very few certified geniuses, I've borrowed everything we do. To the extent any of it is mine, it's only in the way I've adapted certain systems to fit how we want to play.

Basketball, in general, is not a sport where somebody all of a sudden dreams up a new offense. For example, the new trend of smaller lineups with a "stretch 4," a power forward capable of shooting three-pointers, is more of a tweak than it is a radical re-imagining of how the game is played.

My teams always play aggressive defense, but in some seasons we rarely use a full-court press. We'll wait to pick you up until after you cross into our defensive end. In 2015–16, it was just the opposite. I had a smaller-than-usual team. We played with three guards and a stretch 4 in Derek Willis, who was one of our two big men but operated more like a perimeter shooter. I thought we had to play fast to win, so in order to speed up the tempo of games, we pressed a great deal of the time. That wasn't my "system" at work—it was a case of fitting the scheme to the guys we had on the roster.

If I'm known for any one offense, it's the "dribble-drive," which is predicated on keeping the lane mostly open and allowing players to drive it to the hoop and either shoot it from close range, make an interior pass to a teammate, or pop it back out to the perimeter. The player who receives the pass might take the shot, or he might drive it. Sometimes we'll have four or five dribble-drives in a single possession.

The dribble-drive is a fast, free-flowing, and exciting offense that showcases players' individual skills and athleticism but also facilitates team play. I like to coach it. If I bought a ticket to watch a game, it's probably what I'd enjoy seeing as I sat in the stands with a big bag of popcorn. The offense just suits me.

But there are some seasons when we hardly use it at all. It depends on what best suits our players. How do I decide what we run? Part of it, obviously, comes from a base of knowledge and wisdom developed over my three decades in coaching. I can look at my roster and start with a sense of how we're going to play. (I'm not always right, and over the course of a season, it may change.) But even within the style of offense we're running, there are a great many options and it's important to know which of them are really benefiting you.

This is another area in which I can fall back on our metrics. What are our best sets? What are the best actions that we're running? Which players are best at running certain actions? We keep track of all of it. I don't want to get fooled because I've put in something that I think should work based on our personnel—and I'm sitting there thinking that it is working when it really isn't. The business I'm in is like nearly any other: results oriented.

Any coach who says he sees it all and absorbs it all in real time won't have his job for long. It's why you watch the game again on film—and why I'm always going to take full advantage of the story the numbers provide. I want to know what's working so we can keep on doing it—and what's not working so I can scrap it before it hurts us.

Use the Numbers to Promote Certain Behaviors

Lots of fans bury themselves in statistics for fun, or as a hobby. A baseball box score tells a story with numbers, and people my age grew up poring over those things in the newspaper every morning. Now you've got fantasy sites with all kinds of newfangled numbers in all the major sports, and a lot of people are hung up on those. It probably wouldn't surprise you to know that's not my thing.

In our program, I'm interested in numbers that promote certain behaviors. There is a category of numbers that I'd call, broadly, effort statistics. Rebounds, deflections, steals, blocks—those are numbers that typically show energy. But we are able to go much deeper.

How many rebounds you grab in a given game can be a matter of how many missed shots bounced your way. But how many rebounds did you *try* for? Did you box out your man? Did you leave your area to chase a rebound? When your teammate took a shot, did you fight for position and crash the offensive boards or did you make just a passive effort?

Over the course of a season, the player who tries for a lot of rebounds will get a high percentage of them. But if I see a stat sheet after a game and one of the big guys I depend on grabbed just three rebounds in twenty-five minutes, I want to know about that. Was he making the proper effort and the ball just wasn't coming in his direction—or was he letting down?

Again, I can probably see a lot of this stuff myself. But it's useful for me as a conversation starter—or, I suppose, a conversation ender—to look at the statistics that we keep. I'm able to say to a player, "Here it is in black and white. You had seventeen chances to attempt an offensive rebound and you made an acceptable effort on less than half of those opportunities. You say you were trying, but this here shows that you weren't."

Steals are another thing that gets tracked in box scores, but we go beyond that. How many balls did you get your hands on? How many times did you cause an offensive player to change directions? How many times did you close out on a three-point shooter and prevent him from taking that shot, or make him alter it?

These kinds of metrics have a direct relation to what any business does—or should do. There are always going to be factors you can't control—like the price of the goods that you must purchase, swings in the economy that have an impact on your customers, something unforeseen with one of the people who work under you. To me, the most important metrics focus relentlessly on those things you can control, and in our industry, that's effort.

Part of basketball is just math, and we focus on the numbers that matter and how we can make them weigh in our favor. The three most efficient ways to score are (1) from the foul line, (2) near the basket on layups and dunks, (3) an unguarded three-point shot.

The most inefficient shot is the midrange contested jump shot. Our whole goal on defense, then, is to make teams shoot what we call "tough twos"—midrange, guarded jump shots, preferably from just inside the three-point arc. They are low-percentage shots, and even when they go in are worth just two points.

Our kids have grown up seeing the game in a certain way. They've seen the highlight clips of Michael Jordan and Kobe Bryant taking turnaround, twelve-foot jump shots with defenders draped all over them, and are inclined to want to emulate them. That might be a great shot for Michael and Kobe. For mere mortals, even ones as talented as the players I recruit, it's not. I use the metrics to show them that's the shot we want the other team taking.

Let the Numbers Tell a Story

There's a literacy involved in reading the stats and I want to educate my players about that. You've got to look beyond the obvious number and sometimes question traditional assumptions. I'll give you one example: turnovers. Like every coach, I want to limit them. You run down the court and throw the ball to the other team, or commit a senseless offensive foul, or catch the ball while your foot is on the out-of-bounds line—and those are wasted opportunities. It drives you crazy. Too many of those and you lose.

In any given game, I want to keep our turnovers down to somewhere around ten a game—maybe a couple more if it's really fast paced. But what if we play a whole forty minutes and we have three turnovers? I have to examine that, too. It probably means we were playing too slow and not aggressively enough. When you're busting it up and down the court, looking for lob passes that lead to dunks and driving it into the lane, you make some mistakes.

It's not that different from weighing risk-reward in the business world. You can't always play it safe. But if your primary goal is to avoid mistakes, will you ever have a big success? Probably not.

Another example of looking a little more closely at the traditional numbers: On offense, the assist has long been the gold standard of teamwork. Technically, an assist is a pass that leads directly to a made basket—so, for instance, it is a pass into the low post, a perimeter pass to a jump shooter, an interior pass after a dribbler penetrates. Most fans, even some of the real Basketball Bennys out there who know the game, will tell you that an assist is the ultimate expression of unselfishness. The assist man is a guy who gives up the ball. He passes up his own shots. Would it shock you if I said that the quest for assists can, at times, be a selfish way to play? (I'll get back to that in a moment.)

We go a little deeper on how we count assists than what you see in a traditional box score. Just like on rebounds, where a player cannot control in what direction a missed shot bounces and so we track attempts, we understand that a passer cannot control what happens once he gives up the ball.

We keep track of "shots created," and it's more telling than the assist line. If you set up a shooter for a good opportunity—he's open, he can get his feet set, but he misses—you get a shot created. You don't see that in a straight-up box score. (On the other hand, if you throw the ball to a nonshooter twenty feet from the basket and he launches it, for whatever reason, I'm not giving you that. That's a brick created, not a shot.)

We also award a shot created if you feed a player who is fouled in the act of shooting and he gets free throws. What's the difference between that and if he's not fouled and gets a layup? There's isn't one.

Traditional statistics influence how kids want to play. Points, rebounds, assists. If you pile up enough of them—and don't give too much of it back with poor defense—you get playing time. In pro basketball, you'll get paid well.

Now, let's return to what I said about how a player trying for assists can actually equate to selfish basketball—or at least not to the style of play we're looking for at Kentucky. The way we want to play is fast. Get the ball and look ahead. If you've got it and you're still in the backcourt and there's a guy streaking up the sideline—and he's somebody who can do something with the ball on that part of the court—throw it to him. Don't hesitate; just give the ball up.

Maybe this guy is going to take two dribbles and dunk it. Or he'll look across the court and find another open teammate and that guy gets a basket. Either way, the first pass was the key to the whole thing. It got us beating everyone down the court and led to an easy basket. In addition, it sent a message: Sprint as fast as you can to the other end, and we'll get you the ball.

If you look at the stats the next morning, the guy who scored the basket got two points added to his stat line, which he earned by hustling to the offensive end. If he took two dribbles, the kid who passed him the ball might get an assist. If he took three, the passer is probably out of luck.

If it was a second pass that led to the score, that guy is rewarded with an assist. But the key to the whole play was the first pass. It got us going forward and set the sequence in motion. If you look at the stats the next morning, the guy who made that pass got no credit. Zilch. It's the play I wanted him to make, even if it happened to be the point guard with the ball in the backcourt. Just playing the position is not a license to dominate the ball. If there's a guy way up ahead, give it to him!

But it's a hard thing to get players to do. You've got some players with high assist totals who are ball stoppers. On the fast break—or in half-court sets—they want it in their hands. It's how they've been raised and how they see themselves—dribbling out front, scanning the defense. But I want us playing downhill, moving relentlessly and aggressively toward the basket.

This requires, many times, making the pass that leads to the pass that leads to a basket. We call this a secondary assist, or a hockey assist, because in that sport they keep track of the first pass in the sequence that leads to a goal. (They also score a lot fewer goals than we do.)

We're not the only pro or college team to value hockey assists and chart them. It's become common—a prime example of creating a metric to incentivize a certain kind of behavior. It's no different from what any manager would do in the workplace. If something matters, track it. You post the results. If it's a change from how your people are used to going about their work, you explain it. But whatever it is you're seeking, it's never going to matter unless you make it part of your metrics. If you don't do that, then it's just a suggestion.

BEYOND THE ARC

- Use metrics to focus relentlessly on the factors that are in your control. These are often daily, incremental tasks that, when done correctly, add up to big gains.
- If something matters, track it and post the results. This helps make your priorities clear.
- Pay attention to what the stats tell you about risk and reward. If you're not making some mistakes, are you taking enough risks?
- Share the numbers but don't let them become a barrier between you and your people. Really motivated people who want to get better want every tool available to them, and that includes the metrics.
- Lose your ego. Do you want to be known as the inventor of some whiz-bang new way of doing business (that may or may not work), or as a leader who works with the resources at hand and uses them to grow and succeed?
- Do you have a system or way of doing things? Consider changing it up every couple of years or even every year. The best systems are the ones that fit your employees.

6

YOU CAN'T DELEGATE LOVE

This is not a book in which I'm telling the story of a single season, or even a series of seasons. But it is worth looking back at our 2014–15 team—partly because of what we accomplished but even more because that season demonstrates so many things that are at the heart of my leadership philosophy.

I learned a great deal during this remarkable experience about what is required when you find yourself in charge of an unprecedented depth of talent. One is that you must bind the team even closer to each other. Another is that you can and must increase your demands and set your goals higher than usual. All of this, though, must be predicated on tending to your players' long-term goals and aspirations.

One of the things I believe about being a leader is that you can't delegate love. You are at the top of the pyramid, in all regards. What we do on the court, and off it, is all based on caring for each other, and that starts with me demonstrating my own love for those I'm leading.

My house is very close to campus, on a main street in town. I'm not the type who ever wants to live out in the countryside, behind gates. Ellen and I have the players around as much as possible, usually at least once a week. We feed them. When a player has a birthday, Ellen bakes that player a whole tray of brownies. (Some share; some don't.) Over Christmas break, when the team spends a long stretch on campus while classes are in recess, the players come back to our house between practices. I tell them they have to take naps, and they spread out all over our house—on couches, in spare bedrooms, in the basement—and lie down. You look around the house and see huge kids sprawled out in every room, dead asleep.

One of the things that happened during our 2014–15 season is Alex Poythress suffered a devastating injury. During a practice, on a seemingly harmless play with no contact, he planted his left leg and his knee gave out and he went to the floor. It didn't seem at first like it could be that serious. He got up on his own and he could move his knee. But I got a call that night that he had torn his ACL.

Alex, a junior at the time, was our "beast" when he was at his best, an athlete capable of taking over a game with his extreme athleticism. In the previous season, as we made our run to the Final Four, he had some unbelievable blocked shots, just coming out of nowhere to stop sure baskets—he made plays that no other player in the nation could have made. He was a beloved teammate. And then, with one awkward landing, he was lost to us for the season.

We had a team meeting that night and broke the news to the players. Four or five of them cried, and I was emotional, too. Alex and I had been through a lot together. I think that as a leader you have to be strong and steady. But I don't believe in stoicism. Even if you could be successful while being cold and unfeeling, what would it be worth?

What drives me and binds our teams is our deep emotional attachment.

We started out this amazing season with 38 consecutive wins. There were some close games, a couple of overtime victories, and a little luck involved. But still: 38-0 as we set out for the Final Four in Indianapolis. No college basketball team has ever won that many games to start a season, and I don't know if another one ever will.

I am immensely proud of what we did. I'm still hacked off about how it ended, though. Yes, a season is about the journey, the relationships, and the life lessons learned. All of that lives on long after the wins and losses are forgotten. I preach this and I believe it. But we point ourselves toward a destination—the national championship—and that quest does matter. When it doesn't anymore, I'll know it's time for me to get out of the business. It just can't be the only thing that matters.

We did not set out initially to do something historic, but the closer we got, the more we wanted it. There's a national champion crowned every year, but the last one to go undefeated was Indiana in 1976. And back then, they only had to play 32 games. We could have achieved something that was unprecedented. We rarely talked about it directly but it became increasingly impossible to ignore.

If we played a best-of-seven or even a best-of-five series to determine an NCAA champion, we would have won the national title, but that's not how our sport operates—nor how it should. The popularity of March Madness is directly related to its single-elimination format. The tournament starts with great tension and it never lets up through the whole three weeks of play. One bad game and you're out. Not since John Wooden's great UCLA teams in the 1960s and 1970s—which at one point captured seven consecutive national championships, and ten of twelve—has there been a team dominant enough to be considered close to a sure thing.

We were a really good team—and on defense, a flat-out great one—but we proved several times that we were not invincible. We started off the early season, nonconference part of our schedule with some overwhelming wins—beating Kansas and UCLA by a combined 71 points—that got everyone's attention. But we also showed we could be beaten when we didn't give a good effort. Columbia, of the Ivy League (and not even the top of the Ivy League), came into Rupp Arena and led at halftime and we had to scratch out a 56–46 victory. In January, we went to overtime in Rupp to beat Ole Miss in a game we probably had no right winning. A month later we squeaked by with a two-point victory at LSU (the game that I mentioned previously, where Karl-Anthony Towns hung on the rim and gave them life).

The close games, though, were mostly exceptions. Because we were so big and so connected on defense, our opponents usually had a hard time getting to even 60 points. Fifteen of the teams we played could not even reach 50. Kansas managed just 40 points against us, and Providence 38. Our defensive ability—and the pride our kids took in it—provided an unusually big margin for error and allowed us to win even when our own offense was sputtering. If we scored just a normal amount of points, we were probably going to beat you.

Our players felt history building and wanted to be part of it. As we piled up victory after victory and the spotlight on the team kept getting brighter, I felt like it was okay for them to embrace it. Yes, we still had to play each game without looking too far forward. As all coaches love to say, we had to play them one at a time and take care of business. But I've always believed that the kids I coach should note their accomplishments and the milestones they hit. Don't just jump over them and not notice.

In the middle of conference play, I gathered them before practice one afternoon and said, "I'm waking up every morning, thinking I don't want this to end. We're sucking the air out of college basketball. We're outdrawing the NBA in our TV ratings. Everyone's focused on what we're doing because it's so different. I want you to have joy, to embrace it, and not be overwhelmed by it.

"When that last game happens, I'm going to be sad. You're going to be sad. Because we're done. This amazing thing is done. So let's milk everything we can out of it. Live it fully, because it's not coming around again."

BEYOND THE ARC

- A higher level of talent requires that you make demands that may seem excessive or even out of reach. If you're dealing with true champions, they will respond by reaching for goals no matter how high you've set them if they know you care about them.
- Stoicism is highly overrated. As a leader, you should keep your composure—meaning, don't panic—but to hide your emotions or your humanity from your people is a mistake. When something bad happens to one in your group, you're hurting, too, and they should see that.
- Celebrate accomplishments and milestones, but everyone has to understand it's not the end of the road. Conversely, to not take note of important steps along the way is to make the whole march too grim and single-focused. No quest can be about just one thing. A mission that's all-or-nothing invites pressure and, ultimately, failure.

You Are the Caretaker of Their Dreams

A CEO or leader of any type is in the business of persuasion, or you might even say sales. You have to sell your own people on your way of doing things. What is the company culture? What makes it different? If you're going to ask people to throw all their energy and deep thinking and heart into it, what exactly makes it worthwhile? What do you as a company stand for to earn that kind of devotion?

Probably the best writing on this is by Jim Collins, author of the landmark *Good to Great*, who said that the most successful companies build "cult-like cultures around their core ideologies." What he meant, of course, was not that a company itself should become a cult, but that the mission and methods of Company X have to be clearly defined as different from any other company's. The employees must understand those differences and rally around them in order to pull together and reach toward a common goal.

Every season, I teach my team that if they truly buy into our core principles—if they are about each other, rather than themselves—they will each benefit individually. But they also have to know that I have their backs and that nothing I do will be at odds with them achieving their personal dreams.

The other way I sometimes put it is, "First, you have to have your own stuff right." Only at that point can I can bring them together as a team. What I mean is that my players—and any top-tier talents—will not share without first knowing what's in it for them.

This may seem harsh, but it's a reality. Highly talented people have choices. They are not going to choose to land at a place, or stay there, if it means their own futures are diminished. You can't say to them, "Hey, I'm really sorry, but we've got a lot of mouths to feed so you'll just have to step back from the table and wait your turn. Maybe I'll throw you some scraps after everyone else is done eating." It won't work like that.

I was confronted in the fall of 2014 with a problem I had never faced before: too many good players, more than can usually get significant playing time.

We began the season with at least ten guys who were considered elite Division I players, nine of them McDonald's high school all-Americans, every one of whom would have started on just about any other team in the nation. At the publication of this book, nine of them had either been drafted by the NBA or earned an NBA contract—and that number could rise with a couple of them still in college. It wasn't a situation I set out to create, but in the current era, you have to recruit a new incoming class—at least four elite prospects, sometimes more—before you know how many on your current team will opt to leave for the NBA.

I had a group of kids coming in—Karl-Anthony Towns, Devin Booker, Trey Lyles, and Tyler Ulis—and a whole bunch who stayed. The Harrison twins, who a lot of people just assumed would be one-year players, returned for their sophomore year. Willie Cauley-Stein would have been a first-round pick but he came back as a junior, surprising me a bit, but I understood and supported his decision. He wanted to improve his offensive game, and also—having been hurt early in the previous season's tournament run—he wanted to try to reach a Final Four and compete for a national title.

Dakari Johnson returned, even though he probably would have been drafted, as did Marcus Lee, who might have been taken in the draft based just on a couple of breakout games in our run to the Final Four the previous season. And we had Alex, until his injury.

The depth of our talent was ridiculous, and no one thought we would be able to work it out. Even our eleventh and twelfth players—Dominique Hawkins, who had played major minutes in the previous season's Final Four; and Derek Willis, a talented six-foot-nine shooter—were legitimate Division I players, and I didn't know how I'd get them on the court.

I decided we were going to use a platoon system. Two five-man squads. We'd come at opponents in waves, like a hockey team that keeps sending fresh players over the boards. I referred to the next wave of players I sent in not as substitutes—but as reinforcements. Ten guys would get regular playing time; the other two would compete in practice to get into the rotation.

Before I settled on this plan, I talked to some football coaches I respect, including Joe Gibbs and Bill Parcells, guys who were used to playing two platoons, offense and defense. I wanted to know how we could do this and still remain, at heart, one team, and I became convinced that we could.

But by putting in the platoon, I was going against the advice of a great many retired basketball coaches and other experts who held the traditional view that a "short rotation" was the only way to build a cohesive, competitive unit. John Wooden himself had been a proponent of this, and usually played only six or seven guys. In 2010, I called Coach Wooden to ask his advice about my team. We were very young and very talented but I felt offensively we did not execute well. His comment was, "It's hard to cure that when you're playing eight or nine players." He then said, "But I understand that in this day and age, if you don't play guys they will transfer. It's a different day and age now."

My thinking about this unique solution was that I was just changing tactics—not overturning any of my long-held beliefs. And what choice did I really have? It was easy for people on the outside to say that we should just play seven guys, or maybe you can squeeze in eight. But I was like, really, that's what you think? Then what if Devin Booker didn't play? And do you think it would have been fair for me not to play Aaron Harrison, who led us to a Final Four and won games for us with a bunch of last-minute shots? Or—are you ready for this—what if Karl-Anthony Towns didn't play at all? Because Dakari Johnson and Willie Cauley-Stein, they were pretty good, too.

I don't play kids just out of a sense of loyalty. But on the other hand, what they have contributed cannot be a nonfactor. You don't just wipe that away and say, "Thanks for the memories and all you've done, but I've got somebody better now." We ended up winning 67 games in the two years Andrew Harrison was our starting point guard, 33-plus wins a season, which makes him one of the winningest point guards in the history of college basketball. He helped lead us to two Final Fours. By any fair measure, Andrew had an unbelievably successful college career in Lexington.

But Andrew and his twin brother, Aaron, our shooting guard over those two seasons, came with huge expectations. Many of the perceptions about them were unfair, and unfortunately, the twins had body language that did not reflect their true personalities. Their shoulders sagged a little when things weren't going their way. When they were in the game, they were all business and didn't always smile. You would have never guessed that Andrew's teammates considered him one of the funniest kids on the team, but he was. Their teammates loved playing with both of them.

The national media made just about a sport of picking on the twins, and they became convenient targets for anything the media didn't like about me or our program. I tried my best to make light of it. I'd say that if it rained in Lexington or there was a big traffic jam on the highway, you knew who to blame—it had to be the twins' fault. But it was hard on them, though both had the strength of character to stand up to it and keep on competing and improving.

Part of my job is to keep all that outside criticism and clutter away from the team. And just on a pure, competitive basketball basis, I certainly wasn't going to solve our roster logjam by sitting the twins down. They deserved to play, but so did a whole bunch of other guys.

If you're about players first—your people first—are you willing to think outside the box to make sure it works for everyone? Are you willing to be criticized for thinking in those terms? Are you willing to get buy-in from all members of your team because that's the only way to make it work?

BEYOND THE ARC

- Your most talented have dreams. Do you know what they are? Their dreams need to be your dreams, too.
- Your business will be hit with abrupt surprises, some of them of your own doing (I'm talking here of all the elite players we recruited for the fall of 2014—and the surprise of so many elite ones who stayed). You must be willing to pivot and try new things—even to make yourself uncomfortable with methods you never thought you would employ. Otherwise you won't survive.
- Loyalty does matter. The people who brought you and your organization success can't be abruptly discarded or kicked to the curb. If that's what you do, your people will never fully trust you.
- You must always be able to answer the question that your talented people will have: If I sacrifice, what's in it for me?

Leverage Your Own Success as a Tool of Persuasion

It's no small thing to convince a big group of high school all-Americans that they are going to play between 18 and 22 minutes a game and it will work out just fine. College games are 40 minutes in length. On most teams, the starters are on the court for at least 25 of those minutes, and they figure if they're doing well they might get 30 or 35 minutes of playing time. As I wrote in Chapter 1, playing time is the currency of our sport—a kid who is on top of his game expects to be rewarded with as much time as he can handle.

I told my team that they still had to earn their time; they just couldn't expect as much of it. It certainly helped immeasurably that as we began our season, I had already sent more than three dozen of my players into the NBA, most of them as first-round draft picks, a number that was soon to grow yet again. I knew what an NBA draft pick looked like, what the league was looking for, and how they measured and evaluated prospects.

When you're leading elite athletes, you'd better have some background, some street cred, and I've got that. What my kids are looking at is not how many championships a coach has won, but a record of developing and preparing players for the NBA. That's probably not how fans look at it, but I'm telling it from the kids' point of view.

I'm always aware, however, that my voice is not the only one they are hearing. The fact is that people back home have an opinion, and I knew plenty of them would be telling my team that playing half the game wasn't enough. How would they ever get in a groove? Would they even break a sweat? What if they hit three shots in a row? Would I take them out before they could jack up a fourth one? How would they build the kind of stats that would impress the NBA?

No matter what the issue is, I am able to say to my players, "Are you going to listen to me—or to your uncle or barber? Which one of us do you figure has the background to look after your career?"

But this was a little different because I had to admit it was new.

When I introduced the idea of the platoon, I was honest in saying we were going into uncharted territory. "We're all in this together," I said. "What we're about to undertake has never been done before in the history of our game. The only way we can do it is together. Everyone must stay within our circle.

"When we're asking you to play 20 minutes a game, do you trust that the coaching staff has your back? Are you willing to play 20 minutes here instead of 30 to 35 somewhere else and trust that this will actually improve your stock?"

What I knew is that some guys can't play 30 minutes a game and really improve what they're showing to pro scouts. The more they play, the more their weaknesses are exposed. Playing 20 minutes a game, they could go at it with maximum effort for every minute they were on the court.

As coach, I'm not just dealing with twelve players—I'm dealing with twelve kids and their families. As I said earlier, I don't normally like to talk to parents about basketball, but I had to make sure this was communicated to them and that they understood it. They love their children like any other parents, but for them, this basketball thing is not for funsies. These children have a chance of making hundreds of millions of dollars, and they're sharing minutes? If it was my kid, I might have been concerned, too.

I told the players, "I'm not here to coach parents. I'm here to coach you. But you have to communicate with your parents and let them know this is what we're doing. I'm convinced that not only will this work for our team, but every one of you will benefit. Well, you've got to tell your parents that."

I get it that some college basketball traditionalists do not want to hear about the NBA. They may come from an era when the commentators on college broadcasts talked about players going up to the "next level"—because they wouldn't even say "NBA." But that's not the world I live in. My players came to Kentucky because they trusted me to help them fulfill their dream of having a successful pro career, and I have to be true to that. I knew that I had to do some special things to make sure they knew I had their backs and that they were going to be showcased properly.

Between the time the college season ends and the time the NBA draft takes place in late June, the league has for many years held a "combine"—a setting at which players are measured for height, weight, body fat, and some other physical features that matter in basketball, like their standing reach and the size of their hands. They go through interviews. They can take part in athletic testing—how high they can jump; their time in a shuttle run—and five-on-five scrimmages. It's their choice.

A lot of my best ideas come to me when I'm on an airplane, and I was in the air when I thought to myself, I've got a whole roster full of NBA prospects. I could have eight or more of them drafted. Why not invite the NBA into our practice facility at the Joe Craft Center and do our own combine—but instead of after the season we'll do it preseason?

That would give the NBA a baseline look at our players, and later, allow them to see how much the players improved over the course of the season. For me it would be a strong statement that as a program and a coaching staff, the players' goals are our goals. We are committed to them. It showed we had their backs, and got the obvious out of the way so we could go about the business of chasing a national title.

The combine ended up being a home run for the NBA—we had scouts and executives from all thirty teams in our building. We had it so organized that it was to the point of ridiculousness. We fed them. Their parking was taken care of. We gave each team a book so they could compare our kids with the testing that took place over the past several years at the NBA combine in Chicago. (I knew that our players would benefit from those comparisons, both in their measurements and in their performance on the athletic tests.)

It was an absolute grand slam for our kids. All of them helped themselves. ESPN televised it, and they were ecstatic. Who knew that people would tune in to watch a bunch of college kids, preseason, going through something like this? As the season went on, we actually had fewer scouts in the gym during our practices because they had seen what they needed to see—allowing us to focus on the business at hand of chasing a national championship—and we ended up having as many pros on that team as in any other group.

The one complaint I got was that it was a little scripted. No kidding. This was for our kids. I was not going to put them in a position where they didn't look good. As a matter of fact, when we did the backboard touches, Tyler went into the bathroom. With him being five foot nine, I didn't think he was going to impress anyone with how high above the rim he could put his hand.

If You're Given a Competitive Advantage, Milk It

Every four years, college teams are allowed to travel somewhere out of the country in the summer to play a series of games. The players get to experience international competition, and our sport gets exposure outside our borders. The games take place at a time of year when the rules usually prohibit us from practicing as a team. You are allowed to work with players individually, but for very limited periods of time.

We were very fortunate that our opportunity in the cycle was the summer before the 2014–15 season, so it was a chance for our players to get used to the platoon. We went to the Atlantis resort in the Bahamas to play against three teams, and I made sure they were all good ones—the national squads of the Dominican Republic and Puerto Rico, and the French pro club Champagne Chalons–Reims Basket. They were all older than our kids, and almost all of them were pros.

I'm not sure we would have had the same type of season without this trip. It was a head start not just on playing together—but also on being together. The idea of togetherness was something that I stressed right from the beginning, because people told me to be concerned about it. I didn't want the thing to split off into freshmen and returning players—or to have the players on the same platoon relating as an isolated group.

I was able to draw on my NBA experience. I told them that with the best professional teams I've been around, when they're on the road, there are times when all twelve guys go to dinner together. If one guy doesn't go, it's because he has family in town and everybody understands. It doesn't happen every night, but it happens enough that they feel connected. Or they go to the movies, or to a club in a group so they can look out for each other. On bad teams, the plane touches down and everybody goes his own way.

I recommended that they look for opportunities throughout the season to do things together. It could be a meal, or a video game contest. I'd let the upperclassmen organize it. I didn't want the staff to be there. Coaches could be around, but not in the same room.

One of my most important jobs as a leader of the young men who play for me is to model my own behavior and values. I ask them to get out of their comfort zones. Well, the situation with our roster—and the necessity of the platoons—took me out of my own comfort zone, and I didn't mind them knowing that. If I was afraid of trying something new, I could have easily just said, "You, you,

you, you, and you. You're my starting five." And then I'd pick out maybe three others who would play off the bench.

But I couldn't do that. The challenge was to take this situation and not just survive but thrive.

ORLANDO ANTIGUA, ASSISTANT COACH AT KENTUCKY 2010–14, CURRENT HEAD COACH AT UNIVERSITY OF SOUTH FLORIDA

(He was at USF during the 2014–15 season, and the head coach of the Dominican Republic national team we played in the Bahamas.)

We knew that with the amount of talent we were gathering, and a lot of them being alpha males, they were going to have to sacrifice, or learn how to sacrifice. And you couldn't just ask it of one or two guys. You had to ask everybody to sacrifice for the betterment of everyone else. What I'm saying applies to every year, but it probably goes even more so for the season they got off to a 38-0 start, because it was so unusual in the number of guys who needed playing time.

The conversation starts in the recruiting process, so you start setting the table of expectations. You build a relationship from a standpoint of honesty and truth. In the whole recruiting process, maybe some other programs are selling a rosy picture. It's going to be ice cream every day. We're selling you the Brooklyn Bridge. Cal has not had to do that. There's real stuff he can point to and say, "This is our model."

Anthony Davis took the fourth–most shots on the team, and he was the number one pick in the NBA draft. Karl Towns played half the game. He went first overall. That's sacrifice. It debunks the myth that you've got to take every shot and play every minute in order to show the talent you have and showcase yourself for the NBA.

In the first year we were at Kentucky, when we initially took over, we were looking for talent in pure terms. Big, fast, quick. We were lucky. We got kids with good character. But I think as we learned ourselves about what being at Kentucky entailed, we refined it a little. We tried very hard to identify who could mentally handle what was ahead of them.

Could they step in and play immediately, because we had kids leaving? Could they handle the fishbowl that is Kentucky? And could they handle the kind of coaching we needed to give them? When Cal says, "This isn't for everybody," he means some kids are not built for the intensity of what happens on our practice floor and the bright glare of the whole experience.

The success comes as much from weeding out certain guys—and I'm not saying they're bad kids; we just made judgments that they might not be able to handle the whole thing. He has also been able to be creative and step outside the box, for example by bringing in someone like Willie Cauley-Stein.

Willie was a seven-foot-tall football wide receiver who also played basketball. That's how I'd describe him. Not every top program was going to take a chance on him, but we weren't in a position where one top guy has to give us everything. We knew Willie was a superior athlete who would give us defense, and the rest of it, we figured, let's just bring him in and see what happens. And it worked out.

With Cal, the recruiting is not a science—it's more of a feel and a culture thing. Who can play at Kentucky and will they fit in? And the good thing is that I think everyone on the staff, all the assistant coaches, had a mutual understanding of the kind of player we were seeking. Cal set the tone but we all fell in behind it.

Efficiency, Not Volume

Not just this season, but with every one of my teams, I have to change my players' notions about what constitutes a good individual performance. But it was probably even more important with the 2014–15 squad because their numbers were going to be down.

There are limited opportunities in basketball for shots, points, and individual glory. If you go for more than your share, you're probably taking some of mine. Now, I understand how our players might not get that.

We're not like baseball, where there are twenty-seven outs in a nine-inning game and a batting order in which everyone gets his swings. Our game is more elastic. Shoot when you're open. You don't have to wait your turn. Basketball players are conditioned to use their extraordinary talent to get shooting opportunities and then take those shots. As many as they can get. A physically gifted player like LeBron James, who looks to get teammates shots—sometimes seeming to pass up even better ones of his own—is a rare exception.

As a team, we can do some things to increase our overall scoring opportunities—crash the boards and get offensive rebounds; speed up the game by pressing; create turnovers. But what I have to get players to see is that the opportunities are not infinite. There are still going to be only a certain number of possessions each game.

Just about every player I recruit has been a volume shooter who had never even considered the concept of being efficient. He might look at the stat sheet from his high school game and say, "Twenty-four shots. I made eleven of them, including a couple of three-pointers, and I connected on more than half of my foul shots. So that's twenty-nine points. Heck of a game! I'm happy." Mom and Dad were so happy, too, that we all stopped for ice cream on the way home.

I have to show them what in the business world would be called the opportunity cost of each of those shots. Was every one of them a high-percentage attempt? The ones you missed, did someone else on the floor have a better opportunity and you didn't give him the ball? Because if that's the case, the cost of that shot you missed was probably two points—or maybe three if one of our good shooters was spotted up behind the arc and you never even looked at him. So you scored all those points, but did the way you go about it cost us eight points? By not involving your teammates, did you also mess up our offensive flow, cause us to lose a game, and deprive us of an opportunity to grow as a team?

This season was the one that I brought in Joel Justus, specifically to produce a set of statistics based on efficiency—points, rebounds, assists, blocked shots, and a whole range of "defensive playmaking" numbers, with everything calculated on a per-minute basis. That is the way it's done in the NBA. Their games are 48 minutes, but nobody plays all of them, so they don't put that much stock in "per-game" averages. They look at what you made of the opportunities you were given, and extend some of the stats out to what a player would accomplish in 36 minutes—the upper range of what a starter typically plays in a game.

In 2014–15, we had seven players average between 20 and 25 minutes a game. None played more than that. No one scored more than 11 points a game. Our five highest "volume" shooters put up between 6.7 and 9.5 shots a game. By any traditional measure, those are really low numbers. They wouldn't normally project someone as a top NBA draft choice, but in our program we had four players drafted in the lottery, including the No. 1 pick.

I kept feeding our players more information about the metrics and how they are viewed. For example, Joel talked to NBA teams and learned that some of them were tracking rebound attempts by guards. How many balls did they go for? Most guards rarely think about rebounding, and here these teams were tracking attempts, because it told them about a player's "motor"—his effort. Were they willing to go above and beyond the responsibilities normally valued at their position?

With frontcourt players, the NBA was tracking who could finish off of pick-and-rolls, so we started tracking that. I said to Karl, Dakari, and Willie, "You have to be scoring or getting fouled just about every time you roll to the basket and we throw you the ball. The NBA tracks it and we're going to start measuring it, too. That's your money play and you've got to be good at it."

Trey Lyles, a six-foot-ten freshman, was playing small forward for us, not his best position, but we didn't have room for him underneath. He had terrific footwork on the low post, especially for a young guy, but was rarely even getting a chance to use it. His statistics were not what they could have been. But by playing away from the hoop, he was building up his perimeter skills and long-range shooting, attributes the NBA values in a power forward.

I told them, "I'm not afraid to talk to you about this stuff, because your dreams are my dreams. I don't want you to be delusional. I don't want you to look at this and say, 'Well, if I just get more shots or more minutes, then I'm better off.' No! That has nothing to do with how you're being evaluated."

The luxury of having so many elite players was in the energy they could expend in the short bursts they played. One way to make sure they kept their effort at a maximum level was to be clear that playing time was not guaranteed, even with the platoons. If one guy was lagging, I could sub him out—either with someone from the bench who wasn't playing regularly or by giving extra time to a kid from the other platoon.

Or I could just sit all five of the guys down and give the other group more time—and I did that at times. They knew if one group was playing hard and better, they'd be getting more minutes. I let them know, I'm all for you but I'm also one of those guys that love to win. You'd better police yourselves. If there's a guy in your group who isn't playing well, you'd better get on him because he might be holding you all down.

I reached out to Tom Pope, who had success with a platoon system as the coach at SUNY Geneseo, a Division III school in New York. He suggested rotating a platoon out if they gave up more than 6 points before their four-minute shift was up. Giving up just 6 would be 60 points a game, and I figured that would be a big deal with us, as fast as we play. If the other team scored fewer than 6, that shift could stay in the game. The overriding fact about this season was that my team gave me absolutely everything they had. I did a lot of stuff to increase their effort and get our metabolism faster because I knew they were capable of giving more. We judged it all. We evaluated it all. I didn't want anything left on the table.

BEYOND THE ARC

- Use metrics as a tool to educate your people about efficiency. What are the real "costs" associated with the gains they are bringing the organization?
- Make them understand that their own resources of time, energy, and focus might be more effectively put to use in collaborative efforts even if all the credit does not accrue to them. What matters more than the quantity of work is the quality.
- Metrics should be used to inspire people, not to publicly embarrass them.

Finding Different Sources of Inspiration

A season goes by quickly but, in other ways, it can feel long. The players hear my voice day after day for many months, and I understand that it may get tiresome to them and that I've got to switch it up sometimes. There are days when if you listened to me you'd think I was doing stand-up. I've got points I want to make and sometimes it's easier if I've got them laughing.

I'm also cognizant of bringing them fresh information from outside the world of basketball that gives them a different perspective. One day I told them about New Zealand's national rugby team, which is known as the All Blacks and for many years has dominated that sport. What do our kids know about rugby? Not much. (For that matter, what do I know?) But they are interested in winning and in world-class success.

My point that day was to tell them about the habits of world-class teams and what they would have to do to accomplish that:

1. You limit your errors. You are going to make some, but they are not unforced and they usually come from your own efforts to make an aggressive play.
2. You do not just win; you thrash opponents and give them no hope. If you're up 10 points, you don't let them crawl back to a 4-point deficit. You increase your lead to 15 and then set your sights on 20.
3. You enjoy the competition, not just the winning. When a team makes it difficult for you, or a teammate pushes you in practice, you celebrate that as an opportunity for growth.
4. You're never satisfied. If you play well, you're happy but you still find those one or two things you didn't do well and you focus on how to improve. The things you didn't do well upset you. They gnaw at you.
5. You're comfortable enough in your own skin to seek out criticism and coaching from others. You don't feel "less than" when it's pointed out to you in what ways you can improve; you feel empowered. It gives you a mission.

6. You understand that improvement is a process. World-class athletes are always working on adding some aspect to their game. It may be incremental, but over time it keeps them at championship level.

7. You are disciplined in your personal life. Every effort you make to become a world-class athlete can be wiped out with one case of bad judgment. Just like on the basketball court, where you must see the whole floor, you regard your off-court life in the same way. You see the dangers and the possible missteps and steer away from them.

Embracing the Challenge

I've never made a secret of the fact that I don't love the concept of the end-of-season conference tournaments. You've already played thirty games, most of them with at least a couple of days of rest in between them. Now you're playing three games in a row on a weekend. (The teams that finish lower in the standings could play in as many as five straight games.) With the first game of the NCAA tournament less than a week away, the players are wearing themselves out, and it takes them a day or two just to physically recover.

But our fans attend the conference tournament in droves, with so many thousands of them packing the arena that it sounds like a home game for us. Many of them are people who can't get tickets in Rupp Arena, where we play our home games in Lexington. We play for them and we play to win. But the result usually has very little bearing on where the NCAA tournament committee seeds us. (In 2016, we came into the SEC tournament tied for first place in the regular season with Texas A&M; we beat them in the tourney final and still got a lower seed in the NCAA tournament. It made no sense.)

We want to win the tournament, but to be honest, it's not a huge deal to me when we don't. In 2012, the year we won the national championship, we did not win the SEC tournament. We lost to Vanderbilt, though that was the game in which Michael Kidd-Gilchrist volunteered to give up his starting role for a day so Darius Miller, a senior and key contributor who had been struggling, could get himself going. (Michael didn't put it that way—he said he wasn't feeling right—but I knew what he was up to. It was one of the most selfless things a player of mine has ever done.)

The conference tourney in 2014 was a little different. We came into it 31-0. We could have lost and still received the No. 1 overall seed in the NCAA tournament, but our guys were on a mission. They wanted the undefeated season. We defeated Florida, Auburn, and Arkansas. None of the games were particularly close; the average margin of victory was 18 points.

In 2012 I made the statement that I would like to coach a team that could go undefeated. That means winning all forty, including the national championship. People say it's impossible. Why would you put the impossible on a plate of a young player? My answer, as a leader of extremely talented players, is that it is to get them to dream the impossible, to get them to reach for things that they never thought were reachable. Why not? With that being said, we've fallen short every season that I've coached—but we've won 38 games three different times, which is the most in the history of college basketball, including 38 to start a season, which had never happened before. That's all because we were chasing an undefeated season, embracing the challenge and not being afraid of it. Did it add pressure to all of us? Sure. But again, if you have the ability and you want to be a team of the ages that leaves a legacy, that is talked about for the next hundred years, that's what you chase.

Every game in the NCAA tournament feels like pressure, even first-rounders when you're a No. 1 seed playing against a No. 16. No top seed has ever lost in the first round, but who wants to be the first? We were 34-0 at the time. We took care of our first game, beating Hampton, 79–56, and followed that with a little tighter 64–51 victory over Cincinnati.

Our next matchup was against West Virginia, coached by my friend and longtime rival Bob Huggins. His teams always reflect their coach—they're aggressive and in your face. They did some talking before the game, which helped our team worry about one thing: beating them and leaving no doubt that they were not even close to our team. My players were not worrying about going 35-0.

Our team certainly heard all that the West Virginia kids had to say, but they didn't respond in the media. They embraced the challenge and just took care of business on the court. We were up 44–18 at the half and coasted to a 78–39 victory. It was a typical game for us. Our high scorer, Trey Lyles, had just 14 points. Andrew Harrison followed with 13, and three guys had 12. That's balance. We turned the ball over just 10 times.

Our next game was in the Elite Eight round versus Notre Dame—the ACC tournament champions and probably one of the best four teams in the country, which included us. The winner would punch a ticket to the Final Four, and this was the round where it started to get a lot more difficult. The whole game was tight and tense, with a first half in which neither team led by more than 4 points. It was uncomfortable, like we were having a wrestling match in a phone booth.

The second half was more of the same, although we trailed for most of it. With six seconds left, Andrew Harrison got fouled and hit two pressure free throws to give us a 68–66 lead. What followed was probably the signature play of our season. We were a defensive team, and Willie Cauley-Stein was the king of our defense.

Notre Dame inbounded the ball under its own basket to all-American point guard Jerian Grant. As he dribbled down the left sideline, Willie chased him the whole length of the court—boxing him into the left corner. Grant got a shot off, but it was way off. Willie's pursuit of him was a ridiculously athletic play that probably no other seven-footer, pro or college, could have pulled off. My favorite headline the next day: "Willie Cauley-Stein Can Guard Anyone on Earth." It was true.

We were off to the Final Four in Indianapolis, carrying our 38 straight victories with us.

That next weekend in the national semifinal, we came up against a very good and highly experienced Wisconsin team. We had defeated them in the previous year's tournament on one of Aaron Harrison's miracle last-second three-pointers, but they had their whole team back, including center Frank Kaminsky and forward Sam Dekker, both of whom would soon be first-round draft choices.

They were older, but we had plenty of experience, too, including four players who had played in the previous year's Final Four. It was a great college basketball matchup, and the game, like our previous one against Notre Dame, swung back and forth. But we were far from our best.

We got outrebounded and outmuscled. A lot of stuff happened that night, including a go-ahead basket by Wisconsin late in the game that came more than a second after the shot clock expired. We shot the ball well, including 9 of 10 from the foul line, but they were 18 for 22.

Our players will never forget the empty feeling after our loss that night. If I allow myself to think about it, I'm still hacked off that we lost. I've never watched the tape of the game—and never will—because all I would do is think about what I could have done to prevent it and beat myself up over it.

That's just how it is when you're in this business. It's unforgiving. You're rolling along, doing your job, and then the bottom falls out, sometimes before you expect. It's no different in other industries. Something moves in a market overseas, for example, and you're dealing with a completely different reality. If you're in the energy business, to give another example, it could be a new government regulation that hits you—or, in the pharmaceutical industry, a clinical trial that does not go the way you hoped. You get whipsawed.

After the last day of a basketball season, you wake the next morning and feel empty. You're not sure what to do. I know, however, that our 2014–15 season was an incredible period of growth for our players—and for me, as well. Four of them—Karl-Anthony Towns, Willie Cauley-Stein, Trey Lyles, and Devin Booker—would become NBA lottery picks, while six were drafted, tying an NBA record that we had previously set. As for me, I learned how to blend what seemed like an unmanageable depth of top talent—and learned just how hard you can push them when they all feel they are in it together. I also was reminded just how much losing hurts. For everything else about my business that changes, that part of it never does.

BEYOND THE ARC

- Don't be afraid to have extremely talented people reach beyond what they may have believed was possible. The most talented individuals want to be pushed, want to be challenged, and want to achieve something that seemed impossible.
- Adding pressure to gifted people should be fuel that drives them forward. If they fall a little short, they will still reach beyond what they thought possible.
- A CEO or any leader is his organization's chief educator. As such, you define the company and set the goals. If you set them high, your people will follow.
- As much as you're competing against other businesses, entities, etc., you're also competing against yourself.
- There is no such thing as "too much talent." Any leader worthy of the title puts teams together with the proper people to lead them in order to take full advantage of all the human resources. You want to achieve the proper blend of individuals, but you never do so by intentionally bringing in people who will just "fit in" because their dreams are not as big as those of your other highly talented individuals.

7

JUST DO WHAT YOU DO BEST . . . PLAY TO YOUR STRENGTHS

We all spend the first part of our lives trying to demonstrate a broad range of skills and abilities. Close tabs are kept. We are graded, measured, and sometimes sorted.

Some of what you're asked to show, you may be great at; in other areas, you struggle. For example, you are math and science oriented, so in the early grades, you get all your multiplication tables memorized without a problem but you're weaker in spelling and grammar. Or you're a bookworm but sort of allergic to numbers. By the time you get to high school, you're looking at long equations that stretch across a blackboard and your head is spinning. You're miserable, but nobody is going to let you out of it.

Part of this period of life is about discovery—learning your strengths and weaknesses. Nobody wants to pigeonhole a young kid and say you're no good at that, so don't even bother trying. It's important, for obvious reasons, to achieve some minimal level of proficiency at just about everything.

But as you get older, you have more freedom to concentrate in the areas where you truly excel. Academically, you take some core courses in college, but once you're through them, you can concentrate on your major and maybe take some other classes in related fields. You're finally free to pursue your passions. (Even better, you no longer have to stop beating your head against the wall trying to do stuff you're really bad at.)

We celebrate the "jack of all trades" more than we actually reward him. In the work world, a well-rounded individual is always valuable but a person who does just one thing really well is usually more in demand. Very rarely does someone get hired at an elite level because the person doing the hiring decided, You know what, this guy is just pretty good at everything. I'm going to bring him aboard to do B-plus work at seven different things!

It just doesn't work that way. You're usually looking for the person who's an A-plus at his specialty, and the rest of it, you'll figure out.

Excelling at one thing is a calling card—but it's not a stopping point or the end of the journey. Ideally, a person builds confidence off his elite skill and increases his value by adding competencies as he matures. The additional skills you add are not usually something at which you were deficient; instead, you build up from something you were pretty good at to a level of competency that has value in the marketplace. Another way to look at it is that you tap an existing but previously undeveloped strength.

As I go about my business of recruiting, I am always looking for a player who can dominate in an area of our game. It doesn't have to be for the whole game but for a five- or six-minute stretch.

As a rebounder. A shot blocker. A scorer who goes off and can't be stopped. He has to show me that, athletically, he's got that one thing. If he can dominate in more than one area, he's probably a one-and-done lottery pick.

Google, the second most valuable company in the world (after Apple), now employs nearly sixty thousand people worldwide. But when its founders, Sergey Brin and Larry Page, started the company two decades ago, they began with a small group of software engineers who could build and perfect the thing that we all use today—the Google search engine. If you wanted a job there, that's what you had to be: a genius at writing computer code.

What Google found out, over time, was that these people became proficient at other things. They had energy and ambition. They had curious minds. They became managers within the company, leading teams of other engineers, because somebody had to do that. (Google did not hire many MBAs or others with traditional management backgrounds.) A lot of them learned about business and entrepreneurship and went out and founded their own start-ups in Silicon Valley.

But what got them in the door in the first place was their one elite skill. They used it to accomplish their initial success and it gave them a springboard to fill in other parts of themselves.

I don't recruit players because I believe they are one-dimensional, or only have the potential to do one thing well. What I do watch is to see what they would add to our team, not worrying so much about their other areas. Normally someone else on our team will make up for that. Ultimately, they will have to try to build a more varied skill set, either while they're still at Kentucky or after they move on. And most of them are capable of that. But when they struggle, my own go-to move, to put it in those terms, is to get them to focus on what they do best. One philosophy of my program is that we don't harp on weaknesses; we build on strengths.

I say to them, "You don't have to show me everything. What is your identity? What is it that got you on the radar of college recruiters in the first place?" Once they become successful with that, it builds confidence. They can expand it from there.

It helps that basketball is a game in which having just one outstanding trait can get you on a roster and earn minutes on the floor. There are dozens of examples. Certainly, there have been big men in the NBA who could do virtually nothing but block shots and made successful careers from that one skill. I was inducted into the Hall of Fame in the same class as Dikembe Mutombo, who came from the Congo and early in his career at Georgetown was basically just a shot blocker—but such an intimidating one that he disrupted every team they played. Coach John Thompson's defenders could be ultra-aggressive, overplaying opponents far from the basket, because they knew that if any offensive players got into the lane, Mutombo would erase their shots. He made the whole area around the basket a dead zone.

The seven-foot-two Mutombo developed a credible offensive game, but in eighteen NBA seasons, he never averaged more than 17 points a game, and for his career, he scored just 9.8 points a game—which has to be among the lowest (if not the lowest) average of any Hall of Fame player. If you asked an NBA fan what Dikembe did, 99 percent of them would answer: block shots.

Mutombo is somewhat of an exception in that he did that one thing so well he rode it right into the Hall of Fame without really adding another elite skill. (The other thing that distinguishes Dikembe, it should be noted, is that he became a tireless humanitarian, setting an example for the generation of players after him and leading the NBA and the whole basketball community into focusing on good works around the world.)

Bruce Bowen is another player whose career is worth examining. At six foot seven, he was also a defensive specialist. He was not drafted after his four-year career at Cal State Fullerton ended in 1993, so he spent several years knocking around pro leagues in Europe and elsewhere as he pursued his dream of breaking into the NBA.

He knew he was a "lockdown defender," as he would frequently be called, and that was the calling card that finally got him a shot in the NBA. He guarded Kobe Bryant and many of the NBA's other most dangerous scorers—he was named eight times to the league's all-defensive team—and was an essential piece of three San Antonio Spurs' championship teams. Along the way, he developed his shooting, and ranks in the top 25 in all-time three-pointers made in the NBA playoffs—an achievement that no one who saw the young Bruce Bowen play would have ever predicted.

Bowen, in one way, is not a parallel to many of my best Kentucky players. They come to me with probably more raw talent. They certainly have bigger reputations coming out of high school. But there's a lot to be learned from him. One, obviously, is persistence. It's not easy knocking around minor-league circuits and going from one continent to another waiting for a chance you're not sure will ever even come.

But the other big thing is that he knew his identity as a player and stuck with it. Was Bowen what I would call an extreme talent? By traditional NBA standards, maybe not, but his elite talents were his competitiveness and his drive and his ability to sustain those things over a long period of time. Over time, he broadened his array of skills and made himself an even more essential player on a perennial championship-contending team.

BEYOND THE ARC

- Always reach for the individual who really excels at a particular skill, to the point that he's off the charts. Your organization will cover for other areas in which he's just average, or even weak, but you want all of your people to be outstanding in at least one area. Over time, this individual should get better in other facets, but you need to ride the elite skills of your best people.
- Make sure your people fully embrace what their calling card is. They must know: This is what we value you for. We want you to learn new things, but never forget what got you here. Keep doing that one thing and work to make yourself even more elite in that area.
- Don't be afraid to take a chance on people with talents that are not traditional, as we did with Willie Cauley-Stein, who was a very tall football wide receiver in high school but an unpolished basketball player. In fact, if you have a deep talent pool, it should allow you to take the occasional gamble.
- As a leader, have you truly identified your essential strengths and are you putting them to their best use? Have you carved your own role in such a way that your organization is getting the best out of you at every moment—and have you handed off tasks that others can do just as well?

Demonstrated Performance Builds Confidence

I can give players a vision of what I see for them. I'll say, "If you do the following things, this is what you can achieve. This is the best version of you." I'll show them tape of when they've demonstrated it and say, "You see that? That's it! Just keep doing what

I'm showing you right now. Replicate it. Bring that one thing every night."

Or sometimes I'll show them an NBA player who is similar in body type or in some other way and say, "This is what you can become." I'll hit a player with a text and attach a video. Or I'll call him into my office and we'll talk while we look at tape.

I'm dealing with kids from a generation used to watching and touching screens from just about the day they were born, so I'm hitting them where they live. The visual aids help immensely and sometimes make things clear to them in a way that just hearing my voice does not. But you have to keep it brief. You make the points, move on, and let them carry the lessons onto the court.

What I learned a long time ago, however, is that while I can give a player a vision of what he can be, I can't give him confidence. There's no point in me telling an underperforming player, "You're doing great! Don't worry about it! We're still looking for great things out of you!"

That stuff is for the movies. The kid just shot 2 for 9. He turned the ball over six times. He got one rebound and would have had two but he kicked the second one out of bounds. He knows he's not doing great. Of course I'm going to support a kid who is struggling, but if I just try to pump him up in some phony way or give him undue praise, then all I'm doing is making him feel like a charity case. He's so bad that he's inspired pity from his coach.

That being said, I try not to sub a player on a missed shot or a turnover. That doesn't mean I'll let a player miss twelve shots and leave him in or let him turn it over seven straight times. But if a player misses a couple of shots, I might wait until he does something good, like get an offensive rebound or create an assist, before I take him out. Letting him play through mistakes creates opportunities to build his own confidence so as to not have a fear of failure.

What builds confidence is demonstrated performance. My role as a coach is to shape a player and give him an identity that really streamlines who he is at a given moment in time. When he takes the court, he has a mission that is narrowly defined. He knows: Do this one thing, or these couple of things, and I succeed. This is how I build my own confidence. It's how I inspire the confidence of my teammates. And for those looking at me from the outside, NBA scouts and others, it's how I showcase the very best of myself.

I wrote a few chapters back about Julius Randle and how our instruction to him was a matter of keeping it real: Here's what's not working—stopping the ball; spinning into traffic—and why you need to stop. But our teaching was also a matter of defining him by letting him play to his strengths. In other words, here is what will work if you just stick to it and toss out a lot of the extraneous stuff.

Right from the start of the season, there were many games in which Julius was our best player, but there was too much going on in his game. I told him to concentrate on the following things and nothing else: Rebound the basketball. Play defense. Make a strong, definitive offensive move when we pass it to you or make open 15-footers—or give it up. One key was I wanted him to get the ball itself past the defender—meaning no sideways or stationary dribbling. One quick step and go. He was powerful and fast enough to make that happen.

In this way, I carved his game down to its essentials, in order for him to build it up from a position of strength. It's much easier to build your confidence from a position of strength. I have gone through the same process with just about every player I have coached.

You could go back to Michael Kidd-Gilchrist, who as I mentioned was such a good finisher that we made the rule that you had to pass him the ball if he was out ahead on a fast break. That's good game strategy, but it was also a message to Michael: This is who you are right now. You're a greyhound. A ferocious finisher. An unbelievable defender. You can and must add other facets to your repertoire, but this is your calling card for your whole career.

Michael, like Julius, was succeeding early on and had made what anyone would have considered a successful transition from high school to college basketball. They were both good. They both proved why they came to us as such highly rated high school players.

The philosophy of focusing on strengths is even more important when a player is struggling. It's a way of saying, "What got basketball people interested in you? What did they see, and how can we clear away some of the other stuff and get back to basics?"

Alex Poythress came to Lexington as one of the top high school recruits in the nation, and a lot of people expected that he would play just one season for us. It did not turn out that way. In his freshman season, he had flashes in which he looked like that kind of player—starting with just his second college game, when he had 20 points and 8 rebounds in a game against Duke. But he struggled with his conditioning that year and had the additional challenge of performing on a Kentucky squad that struggled. The season was tough for us as a group, and it made it difficult for players, individually, to show their best selves.

Alex was a starter and an integral part of a Final Four team the following season, but then both his junior and his senior years were interrupted by knee injuries. He was extremely unlucky—twice getting hurt at times when he really looked like he was turning a corner. To his credit, he was one of our great academic success stories—a consistent dean's list student who earned his degree in three years and played his senior season as a graduate student.

This is how I broke it down for Alex, the message I kept sending: Just be an elite athlete. He is six foot eight and a sculpted 235 pounds. The muscle was not from the weight room; he arrived with it. He has huge hands and a quick vertical leap. I wanted him to defend, rebound, block shots, make open jumpers, including the corner three, while crashing the offensive boards and scoring off put-back dunks. These are all plays based on effort and athleticism and they were right in his wheelhouse. His injuries took some of his explosiveness away last season, but I still think that when Alex gets back all the way physically he will have a professional career. At the publication of this book, he had just signed a partially guaranteed deal with the Indiana Pacers. The NBA is getting smaller and you can be a six-foot-eight strong athlete like Alex and play the power forward position.

Alex's teammate for two seasons, Andrew Harrison, is another example of a player who needed to hear a very concise message. Like Derrick Rose, Andrew tended to be too hard on himself. I thought it was stopping him from just playing because he feared making mistakes.

Andrew (like Derrick) had the burden of playing point guard for me, which, as anyone who has followed our teams or my career knows, is not easy. With my best teams, I don't call a lot of plays. The players on the court are empowered, as I like to say it. (I'll get to this concept in more detail later.) It's the point guard who controls our pace of play. He has to maintain the very difficult balance of being aggressive about finding his own offense and keeping his teammates involved.

It's a complicated position that requires a great feel for the game. You have to remember, basketball players make nothing but split-second decisions—shoot it, drive the ball, pass it ahead to a teammate. A point guard has the responsibility, as the coach on the floor, of orchestrating the whole thing to my satisfaction.

When I say, "Just do one thing well," you could also substitute another phrase that is common in business: "Keep it simple." I wanted Andrew to play "downhill"—fast and aggressive. Get the ball on the fast break and go. If we are inbounding after the other team scores, get it across half-court in five seconds or less. Use your big body to pressure smaller defenders and get into the lane. Just play like that—at this pace—and don't worry about anything else.

I showed him video of himself when he was doing what I wanted—and also video of Deron Williams, an NBA point guard with a similar build. And I was clear about it. I said, "This is the best version of you and the one I want to see."

Andrew got it, kept improving, and, as I said, ended up in consecutive Final Fours. He just signed a three-year contract with the NBA's Memphis Grizzlies. I couldn't be more happy for a player who deserves it.

They Build Their Own Swagger

One day in early 2016, a friend of mine stopped in at practice and happened to be sitting right in front of where my assistant coach Kenny Payne was putting freshman center Isaac Humphries through a workout. Isaac did some defensive slides up and down the court, then Kenny had him dunk a weighted basketball repeatedly. This is a common drill we do with our big men, and it's really hard. The player has to just keep on going up with a ball that weighs about ten pounds.

Kenny, who played four years in the NBA after playing college ball at Louisville, works with all our players (as does every one of my assistant coaches), but he has a well-earned reputation for having helped develop our big men, including Anthony Davis and Karl-Anthony Towns. Our players love him, and he often serves as a sympathetic ear when they are trying to figure me out—but believe me, he is tough and demanding. One reason our players get better at battling in the post is what Kenny puts them through.

As Isaac's legs were turning to jelly, Kenny was counting down each set. "Three more! Okay, two more! Last one!" Isaac would dunk that weighted ball one more time, bend over from the waist with sweat shooting off him, and rest for a moment. But it wasn't long before Kenny was telling him to get started again.

After a final set of dunks, Kenny sent Isaac over to the sideline, where he had to make his way up and down the court while pushing our strength coach, Robert Harris, who was holding a big foam pad, like a football dummy. Now, Isaac is just the nicest kid you can imagine. He's a talented piano player, and a very hard worker on the basketball court. But this was a killer workout. As Robert kept pushing back against him, making it extra difficult for him to get up the court and finally get a rest, Isaac began to curse at him. Robert pushed harder, and Kenny just stood nearby with a little wry smile.

I could see it from the other side of the court. Isaac kept working and he got through it, as I knew he would. After the practice, my friend said to me, "Did you see that? Man, that was really tough." I responded that it was no big deal. But we do push them to what may look like a breaking point.

I wrote earlier about wanting them to have swagger—supreme confidence but not arrogance. It's a state of being where you know you are the superior player because you've put in the work.

I don't think what I'm talking about here is different in any other endeavor or profession. You go into a final exam with swagger because you've done the reading. Into a sales conference believing you'll win the account because you've researched and rehearsed. Into a closing argument in front of a jury because you've lined up the facts to your benefit and brought the witnesses forward to make your case.

There's no substitute in this world for doing the work. No short-cut. Our work starts with physical conditioning. One of the most famous quotes in sports is Vince Lombardi's "Fatigue makes cowards of us all." There is no way for our players to have swagger without getting their bodies right. And as hard as the work is, it's the most surefire way for them to build their own self-esteem and confidence. You can shoot a thousand shots a day and you might have a game when they don't fall. But if you get your body right, you bring that every night. A bad bounce or an official's bad call can't take away your confidence. Your coach can't take it. It's yours. You built it.

None of my players have ever come into our program physi-cally ready for what is required of them. It's just not possible. They don't come from high schools or AAU teams with the same level of strength and conditioning coaches, or the proper facilities, and they have been so dominant that they couldn't possibly have seen a need to put themselves through the level of rigor we ask.

Our freshmen typically get to campus early in the summer to get a head start academically and begin physical training. By the time we reach the fall, most of them look and feel like different physical beings—with less body fat and more strength, flexibil-ity, and stamina. It's all hard-earned, and we keep at it the whole season.

Great talent should win out most of the time, but to be in lesser shape than the other team is an equalizer. At intense moments of action or at the end of games, they'll get on top of you. Instead of having swagger, you're facing panic. You might as well hand the other team three baskets at the start of the opening tip. Here you go, six points, on us. Enjoy!

I use our superior conditioning as yet another weapon. There are coaches who try to convince their players that their teams are in the best condition. They tell them, "No one's like us. We're the toughest. We're in the best condition." It's a façade. Fake swagger.

I tell my team, "These guys are not in better shape than us. And you make sure they know it." When we play them, I want to make sure we sprint to the bench at timeouts. When the halftime horn blows, we're sprinting again. That is its own kind of demonstrated performance.

BEYOND THE ARC

- Training must be harder than the games. And only crushing, exhausting training builds the confidence that leads to demonstrated performance.
- If you are in a performance-based business, where you must be on the dime at a particular moment—at your best to win the deal or prevail in some other way—are you really properly rehearsing? Are you simulating what we call "game conditions"? Is your training harder than the game itself?
- If you are not succeeding, go back and honestly look at the preparation that led up to your failure. If you had the goods to prevail—the best people, strongest resources, smartest plan—was it perhaps that you did not properly train to win?

Ask a Different Question

A season for me consists of seeking answers to a series of questions and continuing to probe and tweak as we move toward the spring. How do I get each of my players to recognize the best version of himself and then become that? How do I tailor my messages to them? What's the way that we need to play? What combinations of players work and who are the five that I absolutely need on the court at the end of close games? There are times, however, that I have to take a step back and realize that an answer is elusive because I'm not asking the right question.

I wrote about my tug-of-war with Karl-Anthony Towns over getting him to compete down low, near the basket. I went through something similar with Anthony Davis. I always figure that there are not that many human beings in the world who are seven feet tall or close to it. You came out that size for a reason and you shouldn't let it go to waste.

But it's hard to keep banging bodies with other big guys, and the natural inclination—especially for a big player with some guard skills, an outside shot, and still-developing muscle—is to want to gravitate to where there's a little less traffic. You know, I'll just float out to about twelve feet, take a quick fadeaway, and hope it goes in so the coach doesn't yell at me.

I get it. It's easier. So I have to just keep telling them, "Get back in there! Use your legs and your butt and anything else you can get away with and carve out your territory." My answer, basically, to how I'll get them to play the way I want is to teach them the skills they need—and then to just keep demanding it and making clear that anything less is unacceptable. That's just coaching.

For more than half a season, I went through the same battle with Skal Labissière, a seven-foot freshman on our 2015–16 team. I wanted him to embrace his height, all eighty-three inches of it. That's not a normal size. When you combine it with his athleticism, it equates to extreme talent. So I'm going through just about the whole season thinking, Let's just get this kid stronger and tougher. Teach him to play with his back to the basket. I've done this before in my coaching career and I need to just keep hammering away at it until I get what I want. The way I sometimes put it is that it's my will or theirs—and my will is stronger.

But Skal's journey to college was different from any other player I've ever had. In fact, it was nothing short of miraculous. When he was thirteen years old, his city of Port-au-Prince, Haiti, was struck by a massive earthquake, magnitude 7.0, made even worse by the fact that the typical structure there was the opposite of earthquake-proof. It's a very poor country, and the buildings were not well constructed. Just about everything crumbled, including Skal's house.

At least 200,000 people died. Skal was trapped under rubble with his mother and brother, and it took hours for them to be rescued. His legs were injured and it took some time before he was walking normally again. He came to the United States not long after and settled in Memphis, where he had to learn a new language and new customs.

He had not played that much organized basketball to that point, and the first high school he attended did not play a highly competitive schedule. When he attempted to change schools for his senior season, his eligibility to play got caught up in some state rules regarding transfers, and he was not allowed to compete that year.

Every player entering a program like ours goes through a period of adjustment. The game is faster, the opponents bigger and stronger. We're usually one of the youngest teams in college basketball, and sometimes I've got seventeen-year-old freshmen going up against twenty-two-year-old seniors. I don't care how good you are, it's going to take you a little while to figure that out. Over time, size, athleticism, and skill will win out over experience. But it doesn't happen right away.

Skal was in a category all his own because he arrived in Lexington as such a raw prospect. Not only was he thin and lacking strength, but in terms of the number of games he had played, he was still back in high school. He had made a big impression and created a lot of buzz in some practice sessions and individual drills at post-high all-star games, and there was a reason for that: He had spent a lot of time being coached individually, more so than he had in up-and-down five-on-five games.

His talent was extraordinary—great quickness, a quick leaper, and a soft and accurate shooting touch. If you walked into our gym and watched him shooting by himself at practice, your eye would be drawn to the sight of this big kid just feathering in jump shot after jump shot from what we call the "elbow"—the spot to either side of the foul line. If he took 30 of them, he'd probably hit 25, or maybe more on a really good day. How often do you see young players his size shoot like that? Almost never.

And it wasn't just the accuracy. Basketball is not ballet but still there's a beauty to it. People who are really into the game, including scouts and executives who make personnel decisions, are taken by athletes who have a certain fluidity of movement. If you designed how you wanted a big player to shoot a basketball—easy motion, high release, off the fingertips, nice backspin—it would look like Skal. Somebody taught him that but when you watch it, it's pretty clear he's a natural. That potential was just in him.

He started out the season playing well, and probably fooled us a little bit. In just his second game, he scored 26 points against New Jersey Institute of Technology, hitting 10 of his 12 shots and all six free throws. He added four blocked shots. He had three more games where he scored in double digits in the season's first month.

But when the competition got tougher and we started facing teams with players who were as big, and a lot stronger, everything changed and it happened quickly. He started getting pushed off his position down low. We'd give him the ball and sometimes it would just get ripped right from him. If he did get a shot off, he was off balance or his footwork wasn't right because he could not stand up to the physical play.

There were times he played 20 or 25 minutes and was able to

grab just two or three rebounds. I'm sure we had fans watching and saying to themselves, "I could get two rebounds in twenty-five minutes!" That's not really fair (they couldn't) but they were not wrong in thinking there were moments when Skal was in over his head.

He fell out of the starting lineup and when he did enter the game I sometimes quickly subbed him out for the sake of the team. (When you tell players they must compete for minutes, you have to really mean it. Nobody gets them as a guarantee, no matter what his reputation or long-term potential may be.)

By the time we hit the heart of our conference schedule, Skal was not playing a lot—sometimes fewer than ten minutes a game. An even younger player, Isaac Humphries, a first-year kid from Australia, had taken some of his court time. He didn't have Skal's tools but he had more muscle and more fight. And I was playing Derek Willis in one of the two frontcourt spots, which I had not planned on at the start of the season, but he gave us another shooter, which we needed.

I knew it was frustrating for Skal as well as humbling—after all, he had been considered one of the top incoming freshmen in the nation and was predicted to be among the first couple of picks in the NBA draft. I never questioned his character or his fortitude. Look at what he had survived in Haiti before he got to the United States and found his way to Lexington. That took a lot more grit than anything we were asking him to do on the court.

It was ridiculous to think that he was not tough or resilient. His problem was mainly inexperience and a lack of strength. Even when he had the power to clear space for himself, he didn't really know how to do it. We tried to teach it but he was having a hard time taking it from the practice court into games.

With him struggling, and sometimes barely playing at all, I had to look inward and ask a different question. Instead of, Why can't Skal post up? I had to consider, What's my part in this? Am I leading him in a direction that he just can't go right now and not helping him or the team? Is there a different course, and what is it?

There's a point at which you can't drag someone to where they don't want to go, or can't go. You have to give them something to succeed at. To go back to what I touched on at the beginning of this chapter, it's like if you have a student who's stronger in English than math: You have to build on that strength. Okay, we're going to read more books, and we'll give you advanced books. We're not giving up on the other thing, but we will build confidence off your strong point.

In practice, we started using Skal a different way, giving him more "pick and pop" opportunities—he would set a screen for one of our perimeter players, and just float out to the elbow. If he got the pass, we encouraged him to shoot his smooth midrange jump shot. The pressure to be something else was lifted. The more his shots fell, the more his confidence grew and the more the rest of his game started to come around. He rebounded more balls and was more active on defense. He is as natural a shot blocker as he is a shooter, and he started going after more balls.

The other thing I did was take blame publicly. I said I had been coaching Skal the wrong way and trying to make him into something he wasn't. I meant that, and I also wanted to take yet more pressure off his shoulders and give him a fresh start—this time, with the freedom to play to his strengths.

His teammates, who loved him, noticed his transformation in practice. Before a game against Florida on March 1, I said to Tyler Ulis, "Should I start Skal?" He said yes, without hesitation, even though Skal hadn't started in weeks. (I had come to rely on Tyler not just for his play but also as something almost like a player-coach.)

In that game, in Gainesville, which is a very challenging environment for any visiting team, Skal scored 11 points and grabbed 8 rebounds in just 15 minutes of playing time. It was by far his best game in months. He was even better a few days later, at home in Rupp Arena against LSU—18 points, 9 rebounds, and 6 blocked shots. He absolutely dominated the game—and did so against the eventual number one pick in the draft last season. Anytime LSU got the ball near the basket, they were looking at Skal's long arms, and he altered at least as many shots as he blocked.

Our fans, by and large, are kind to our players. They don't boo, but sometimes, when the players struggle, you can sort of hear that low murmur and you know they're dissatisfied. That had been happening with Skal when he seemed passive and couldn't get his hands on rebounds. But just like I don't give up on players, neither do our fans. They were going crazy watching Skal that night, and it was just great after what he had been through.

Skal started for us in the games we had remaining. He didn't have another performance like the LSU game, but he was better. I knew that he was likely to want to go to the NBA. His family needs his help. I get that college basketball fans rightly wonder, How is it possible that a player who struggled to get on the floor for his college team could even think about turning pro? And why would he be drafted? If he had a great attitude and solid skills for his size, which he did, we knew the NBA would overlook his college growing pains. They are focused solely on potential.

By reconsidering the approach with Skal—asking a different question—we helped our team a great deal. We were really good at the end of the season. He gave us another scoring threat, helped spread the floor, and was a defensive presence. And he helped himself.

BEYOND THE ARC

- Your role as a leader is to keep probing and keep asking new questions until you have sparked the talent that caused you to recruit this person in the first place.
- Talented individuals in almost all cases want to perform to expectations. You cannot blame them when they don't. It may be that you have to alter your own approach.
- Within your organization, finding ways for your most talented individuals to excel and flourish is your goal, even if you have to change your approach.

They Are Each on Their Own Path

One of the most important things any leader has to understand—and one of the most difficult—is what you can control and what you can't. Your tendency is to think you can orchestrate everything. You're the maestro. That's why they put you in the job. Even when you know it can't really go that way, you drive yourself crazy trying to find all the hidden buttons—the ones you can press to magically solve your most stubborn challenges.

The fact is that I can control a lot about the team and our program. I pick the lineups and make the substitutions and decide what offenses and defenses we run. We need a basket late in the game and are taking the ball out from under our basket? I've got several plays for that. I think just about any coach will tell you that the X's and O's are the easy part.

One thing I can never lose sight of is that the train is always moving. I'm running an advanced class, strictly for the gifted and talented. If I wait for some guys, I'm holding the others back.

That's the deal when you sign up to go here. Come in ready, and keep up.

Is that unfair to some kids in the beginning? Probably. But I've never had good players get left behind—if they struggle in the beginning, and they're worth their place here, they catch up. Anyone buried by expectations was not going to help us anyway. You've got to be alert and wide open to learning. Our practices move fast and our games move faster. The season flies by. Careers here at Kentucky, for a lot of our players, are fast. Over in a blink of an eye.

What I've had to learn over the years is that each of my players arrives with a personality that is rooted in his genetics and family history. I can help them create new habits. We can and must teach them new skills, which they need to survive at this new level of basketball—and the one they aspire to. We give them a better understanding of game strategy—how to play at certain times based on the score and clock. But what I can't do is change their inner wiring. I've got no button to press for that. I can only seek to understand who they are and work with them.

I wrote about Skal, who is lavishly blessed athletically but for reasons having to do with his temperament and history may take a little time to reach his potential. But he was drafted twenty-eighth in the first round by the Sacramento Kings (via the Phoenix Suns), and the franchise, based on its first look at him, already feels like it got a steal.

In some ways, Devin Booker is the opposite. He was, somewhat unfairly, I'd say, considered just an average athlete coming out of high school—not explosive or superfast. At six foot six, he was a terrific shooter but not highly regarded as a ball handler, playmaker, or defender. But his wiring is totally different from Skal's. Devin is confident and laser focused; he came to Lexington convinced that the opinions of the so-called experts were dead wrong, and he was determined to prove it.

I had to respect these aspects of Devin. If he had a chip on his shoulder about the way he was regarded, I had to have a chip on my own on his behalf. My ambition for him had to equal his own ambition. If he was in a hurry, I had to be in a hurry for him. I've joked about players saying to me, "But Coach, you just don't understand my game." Devin believed the whole world did not understand his game and he was on a mission to set them straight.

Devin benefited from an upbringing in which he was drenched in basketball. Melvin Booker, his father, had an illustrious collegiate career at Missouri, averaging 28 points a game in his senior season. He was the Big Eight Player of the Year in 1994. Despite that, he went undrafted by the NBA, played in the Continental Basketball League, and then played for short stints in the NBA with Houston, Denver, and Golden State. After that, he played a decade of pro ball overseas in Italy, Russia, and Turkey.

That all equates to a sort of basketball school of hard knocks. Only the strong survive that kind of hoops journey.

Devin, meanwhile, was being raised in Grand Rapids, Michigan, by his mother. In the summers, he stayed with his dad in Moss Point, Mississippi. When Melvin finally came off the road, Devin was entering high school, and the family decided he would move to Mississippi and live with him. Sometimes Devin played in pickup games with his father and his father's friends—against grown men who made up for what they had lost in quickness with smart, very physical play. He had to learn to stand up to it. Melvin was strong and a force in his son's life as a father and mentor. (The first time I went to meet with Devin and Melvin, I learned that I had coached Melvin after his senior year at Missouri. Melvin looked at me and said, "You know you coached me, right?" And I said, "What?! Where?" He said the Buckler Challenge. I vaguely remembered, but it was a while ago, so I followed up with, "Did you have fun?" He said he did. I said, "Did I let you shoot it all the time?" He said, "You let us play." At that point I'm thinking, Phew!)

I was very lucky in that Devin arrived with an already accelerated basketball education. His dad did not enable him or pull punches, and he told his son the truth. Melvin Booker knew enough about basketball to see the same weaknesses in Devin's game that others did, and he set out to correct them.

At the end of Devin's senior season, several of the scouting services had Devin ranked as just a four-star rather than a five-star prospect, what the top guys get. He was considered somewhere around the twenty-fifth-best player in his class, which isn't bad but doesn't project to a fast path to NBA stardom.

I read somewhere that Draymond Green, a second-round pick of Golden State but now an all-star, can recite from memory the name of every player who was picked before him. Devin has that kind of mentality. If he feels snubbed, he uses it. In the summer before he arrived on campus, Devin played in the Nike Global Challenge in Washington, DC. He was one of twelve players on the South team, which made him one of forty-eight from the United States. They played teams from around the world. He played no more than five minutes a game at the end of noncompetitive games, sometimes called garbage time. No question he could name the other eleven players on his team and probably the other forty-seven American players who played more minutes than him, all of them his age. He didn't like sitting on the bench in that tourney and he didn't forget it.

If that kind of attitude just comes out as bitterness, it's no good. For guys like Devin, it's fuel. He has soft facial features, a choirboy look, but he's tough as hell. He'll talk junk to you on the court. He won't back down physically.

I know that when Devin committed to play for us, he had no idea how crowded a roster—and backcourt—we would have. He expected, like just about everybody else, that Aaron and Andrew would be one-year guys and off to the NBA. I know it bothered him, but he has a way of channeling everything into a positive.

My players are not normally big watchers of basketball tape. I'll give them some stuff of upcoming opponents, but it's limited. They're not going to watch an hour of scouting video. What they like to do is watch their own highlights.

People sometimes compared Devin to a young Klay Thompson, the all-star shooting guard on the Warriors. They're about the same height, both thin-framed, and both are long-range shooters. I didn't have to bring tape of Thompson to Devin; he was already watching it. That's its own kind of talent. He was like, "That's me. That's my future if I can model my game after his."

I've had others like him. Brandon Knight was one. Their drive is beyond the norm. It's almost like, where did this come from? It's nonstop. And they have an energy level that's endless. Those two things are connected because they feel like they should always be doing more. They'll be in the gym at midnight. Neither of these guys, when you look at them physically, seem like they should have been a lottery pick, but both made themselves into that.

What I have to realize as a coach is that these guys need something from me, too—just as much as the others do. I might not have to motivate them as much, but they need my affirmation of their work and ambition. I might have to monitor them and make sure they don't wear themselves down physically. Most important, they need to know I'm in their corner. I'm their ally in proving the doubters wrong.

Devin was selected by the Phoenix Suns with the thirteenth overall pick in the 2015 NBA draft, and in his rookie year exceeded any projections—except perhaps his own. He was still only eighteen years old when the season began, the youngest player in the whole league. At first, he did not play a lot, but injuries to two others in the Suns backcourt—my former players Eric Bledsoe and Brandon Knight—gave him an opening. In the season's second half, he averaged 18 points a game. Six times he scored 30 or more points. He became the fourth-youngest player to score 1,000 total points, behind LeBron James, Kevin Durant, and Kobe Bryant.

Most significantly, he showed elements of a well-rounded game I'm not even sure I knew existed—or at least I didn't think it would emerge so quickly. Devin had to play some point guard, and in a game in March became the second-youngest player (after LeBron) to total 11 assists.

At the end of the season, Devin was voted onto the NBA's all-rookie team—a remarkable achievement considering he was not even considered anywhere near the top five kids coming out of high school a year earlier. (Karl-Anthony Towns was also on the all-rookie squad; Willie Cauley-Stein was selected among the second five.) Think about it: Devin was our sixth man and never even started a game and is now considered one of the bright young stars of the game.

W hen I say that each of them is on his own path, by the way, I want to make clear that the path is not always to the NBA, or at least not quickly into the league. We have had plenty of players who stayed for three or four years. (All who stayed for four earned their degrees.) This program is for them as well, and each has reaped the academic and social benefits of the college experience.

Right now we have Derek Willis and Dominique Hawkins, both of them in their senior seasons. They both had to fight for playing time their whole careers with us, and both earned it and have made major contributions. I think they'll both play basketball somewhere after they leave Kentucky. Darius Miller is yet another who is on his own path. He played four years at Kentucky, and while he's still trying to get a permanent foothold in the NBA, he's played in the league for parts of each of the last three seasons.

Because of the extreme talent we attract—and the kids who go quickly to the NBA—it may seem to some that players like Derek, Dominique, and Darius are outliers. They are not. They are on a normal college path like most kids at most other schools. They bided their time their first couple of years, worked really hard to improve, got some experience their junior seasons, and now are ready for big senior years. The only difference is that it doesn't seem like normal path at Kentucky because of some of the draft numbers we've had, but that's not fair to those kids who have improved and have earned their time. They have been an essential part of our success, and I take great pride in the progress they made during their time with us.

DEVIN BOOKER ON HIS KENTUCKY EXPERIENCE

Honestly, I didn't anticipate the way the roster was constructed. Like everybody else, I thought the Harrison twins would leave. That was part of my decision, that I'd come in with Tyler and we would play together in the backcourt, hopefully as starters. And also coming in with Karl and Trey Lyles, it was a great class.

But Cal called after Andrew and Aaron had made their decision and he said, "Trust me. Everything is going to work out. Believe me." I thought, All right, if you're saying it, I'm going to believe it, but at first it was indeed hard to believe. That's like ten McDonald's all-Americans on one team. I didn't know how it was going to work.

He started the platoon system—five come in, five go out—and it was strange to us. We talked about it among ourselves. None of us came up in a system like that—it's not really done anywhere—and I don't think anybody liked it at first. But he said, if one of us eats, everybody eats. And he stayed true to his word, and we all began eating, and it worked out well for us.

The reason I went to Kentucky is because I realized that's what the NBA is going to be like. It's going to be a lot of great players out there. Everyone is going to have to share and play the right way at all times. That's what's expected of you at Kentucky. They treat you like pros. Everything is professional—the way we take care of our bodies, our nutrition, our training, everything. It's the blueprint to get to the NBA.

The recruiting process was straight-up honesty. You get recruited at other places, you get told, you know, "You'll be the face of our team. Everybody will love you here," but Cal was the only one saying, "You're going to have to come in and earn it." He told me that even before everybody decided to come back. So when they came back, it was a surprise, but in another way it was consistent with what I had already been told—that nothing will get handed to you. You can't say, "What about my guarantee?" because you didn't have one.

My dad and Cal are similar. Tough love. They're going to get on you and hold you accountable. There were times when I did feel, I hate this guy. He's holding me back. I got mad at him, and to be honest, I think he expects you to be mad sometimes. He doesn't mind. He expects that passion. But I never felt that way for long because you can see the results as the season goes on. You're getting better in all facets of the game. That was my stated goal, so I was like, All right, this is what I signed up for. Just keep pushing and working and competing. That's all he's asking and it matched up with what I wanted.

BEYOND THE ARC

- Do not compare extremely talented people. They are all on different paths and built differently.
- Do you expect your team to react like you would in all situations? If you do, you will be disappointed.

8

EMPOWERING YOUR TEAM

I have not written these chapters in order of importance, but if I had, this one might be number one. There is nothing more important. Empowered individuals take initiative and responsibility. They see around corners, anticipate problems, and formulate solutions. When they make a mistake, they own it and try to fix it. They don't blame and they lift up others.

Are Traasdahl, the CEO of a global advertising firm, has an instructive (and very funny) way of talking about empowering people to solve their own issues. People come into his office with a problem of some kind, or as he says, with "a monkey on their shoulder." When he was a less experienced leader, he tried to be the one to solve all their problems. His employees just threw off what was bothering them and walked out the door, leaving him with an office full of problems.

Not only did that give him too much to do, but it took away from those people the responsibility—and, in fact, the privilege —of learning to solve their own problems. Over time, he realized that his goal should be "when they walk out of your office, they're going to take their monkey with them."

I put it to my people in a slightly different way but the point is the same. I say: If you come into my office you've got to take stuff off my tray. If you put stuff on my tray, why do I need you? When my staff leaves my office, I should be able to go home.

One common myth is that the boss (or coach) "empowers" people. I don't think that's how it goes. In my mind, your people already have power inside them—they just have to find it within themselves and use it, rather than shirk it off. "People have to empower themselves," executive coach Marshall Goldsmith writes. "Your role is to encourage and support the decision-making environment, and to give employees the tools and knowledge they need to make and act upon their own decisions. By doing this, you help your employees reach an empowered state."

Be Random Yet Organized

General George S. Patton once said, "Don't tell people how to do things, tell them what to do and let them surprise you with their results." That's a pretty good philosophy for the leader of any kind of enterprise. Your people have to own their own work, and they never will if you're standing over them micromanaging every move.

I'm lucky in that basketball is a naturally empowering environment. I can't possibly call every play. I can't dribble or shoot for them. The whole thing is too free-flowing and fast-moving. One of the things I always say is that as a team, we want to be "random, yet organized."

What does that mean? I'll start with the second part of it first. When we take the court, we are organized around an agreed-upon set of principles. We play fast. We employ an array of offensive sets, lining up our guys at certain parts of the court, but we run what I call "actions" rather than plays. We respond to the defense and to our players' own sense of energy and creativity.

There are times we don't run anything at all. I tell them "just play"—which means get a defensive rebound, a block, or a steal and then just run. If there's not a shot off a fast break, we're not going to stop and set something up. Someone can make an aggressive play that leads to a scoring opportunity. Maybe we'll have one of those "hockey assists"—a pass that leads to a second pass that leads to a hoop. But it will be naturally occurring.

The random nature of the way we play is that we have multiple options built into everything. We're not robots. We're unpredictable. The more random we are, the greater our competitive advantage because we're not predictable. But it requires each one of the five players on the court to be empowered.

Move into the space that the flow of the game directs you to. Find your teammate if he's open. Take the shot if you're open. We want to be flexible enough to pivot and move as the situation calls for it. Whatever choices you make, they'll be right as long as you're being unselfish, as long as you're playing hard, and as long as you're playing in balance. Our principles should have you moving to areas of the court that maintain proper floor spacing, but you have to be dedicated to executing that correctly.

On defense, stay in front of your man—but if one of your teammates is beaten, cover for him. If the ball finds the man you left, someone will cover for you. That's empowerment and it's trust.

We sometimes refer to this kind of defense, where we're chasing the ball and closing out on open shooters, as "scrambling"—meaning that we are all running around like crazy, each player helping out the others. It's not much more complicated than that. We don't want to give up an open three-point attempt or a layup.

If we scramble hard enough, the other team won't get any decent shot off before the thirty-second clock expires.

But you can't have a player just thinking about his assigned task—meaning the man he was guarding. That guy doesn't play team defense. He takes what seems like a safer route. What, me? It wasn't my guy who scored. On an empowered team, every player feels a responsibility to the whole.

All of this stuff I just described, I believe, could also illustrate how you would want a certain kind of business to operate: nimble, quick to respond, able to deal with uncertainties, and empowered enough to solve problems on its own. Your competition can never be quite sure in which direction you are headed.

An empowered team organizes itself around a small set of easily understood themes, and the leader defines those themes. Some people have called me a salesman, and I know it's probably not always a compliment. But salesmanship is one of the hallmarks of leadership. In sports, we use the shorthand: Has the team bought in? Are they buying what you're selling?

My themes, or messages, change subtly from year to year, depending on the makeup of the roster. In 2014–15, when we had such a depth of talent, I would say: "Everybody eats," meaning we all had a place at the table. We would share in such a way that everyone benefited.

The following year, I said we would play "positionless" basketball. That was born of necessity but it was also the direction in which the NBA was moving. We were smaller than normal and played a three-guard lineup most of the time. We often had no traditional center on the floor. The guards had to rebound, and one of them often had to defend a bigger player. My ideal team would average a height of six foot nine; all of them could dribble, pass, shoot, and play multiple positions defensively. We could switch on defense and take advantage of other teams' weaknesses without substituting.

The broader theme is shared responsibility—which is closely related to empowerment. You don't just stay in your lane. You are expected, and empowered, to cover for your teammates—maybe because you're so similar. I always keep our focus on us, rather than the competition, and I would argue that is sound strategy for any business and is its own form of empowerment. We control our outcomes rather than get distracted by what's happening on the periphery.

BEYOND THE ARC

- Empowered individuals allow organizations to be nimble and quick. They can turn on a dime because the people have enough responsibility to respond without first going up a chain of command to seek permission.
- The empowerment facilitates personal development, and often a satisfactory and fulfilling work life for the individual. But it does just as much for the team.
- The faster a team can change directions, and the less predictable it is, the more formidable a competitor it becomes in the marketplace. Competitors can never be sure what's coming next.

Ignore the Barking Dogs

Winston Churchill had a great quote that relates to this: "You will never reach your destination if you stop and throw stones at every dog that barks." Exactly. Our team has a high public profile in an era of wall-to-wall social media. There are lots of barking dogs out there.

Whatever we do—whatever moves I make—someone in the media will offer criticism. I wrote earlier about playing two point guards, John Wall and Eric Bledsoe, together. Plenty of people said at the time that wasn't possible and I'd be failing the team and both players.

Sometimes the critiques are offered by "experts" just trying to be smart. Other times it's people wanting you to fail. It was the same when I decided to use the two platoons. I am quite sure that it was used against us in recruiting. "Don't go to Kentucky; you'll only play half the game." All I can do is ignore it, and tell my players to do the same.

I've got a big sign in my office that says COACH YOUR TEAM. And that, too, is about empowerment. Everything else is a distraction—all the clutter, all the hearsay, all the opinions. It's all a distraction. This helps empower me to not worry and do what I do best, which is coach my basketball team.

Similarly, I tell our players, "Don't relish in others' misfortunes." That, too, is a distraction. (It's also probably bad karma. If you enjoy the problems someone is having, pretty soon you'll have some of your own.)

Your most worthy competitors are, simply put, trying to beat you. And they are capable of it. One of the best ways to allow it to happen is to be too focused on what they're doing, and get bogged down in that—rather than pushing the boundaries of your own performance. Constructive criticism doesn't bother me, but destructive criticism does, and most of that is agenda driven.

I have no idea how to estimate the volume of stuff that is written about us, and me, during the season and how much commentary there is on TV. It's a ton. And there's plenty in the off-season, as well. I try to model for my players how to tune it out. I'm certainly aware of some of it, and need to be as the leader of our program (in fact, I have people in place to filter some of that stuff down to me so I'm aware but not overwhelmed with it and can do my job). If there's something I hear or read that I absolutely must respond to because it is factually incorrect or has the potential to hurt our program—or if someone brings this material to my attention—I will do so.

But I never react out of anger. I will compose a tweet or something for my website but I don't just put it out there. I run it by a series of people I trust—three or four of them—before it ever sees the light of day. I'm that cautious, because in this age of social media, I think you have to be.

Everybody Has a Different Seat on the Bus

My team includes not just the players but people throughout the athletic department and university who support us in various ways—including DeWayne Peevy, the deputy director of athletics and our administrator for basketball; our trainer Chris Simmons and strength coach Robert Harris; my longtime secretary, Lunetha Pryor; Chris Woolard, associate athletic director of basketball operations; Michael Stone, longtime academic counselor; Eric Lindsey, the associate director of media relations for basketball; Deb Moore, the assistant media relations director; and Metz Camfield, the editor of CoachCal.com, my website. My closest collaborators are my assistant coaches—Kenny Payne, John Robic, and Tony Barbee, as well as Joel Justus. It's a big team and I need the help of every one of them. My goal is to have every member of the athletic department staff and my immediate staff feel our success would not have happened without them engaged in the mission.

One of my favorite business authors, John C. Maxwell, writes that the first person a leader must manage is himself. I want to have the same energy and commitment as I did when I was a younger coach, and I've found one way to do that is to keep to an established and disciplined routine.

I get up early and I go to Mass most mornings. I'm not trying to tell anybody what to do, and it's not my proper role or my inclination to proselytize, but this is my time to reflect. I usually go from church to a Dunkin' Donuts, where I have coffee and shoot the breeze with a few buddies who meet me there every morning. (So just about every morning by 9:30 a.m., I've prayed, I've laughed, and I've solved world problems. That's a pretty good start to a day.)

During the season, I go to my office and spend a couple of hours on practice preparation. I'll meet with my assistant coaches and, often, whatever players might walk through the door. I try to exercise for at least forty minutes and have started lifting weights.

I recruit during the season, but I never miss a practice session. We must give our team one day off a week, so that's the day I go out on the road. But it's a grind, because I'm on a plane going out to a high school game somewhere, sometimes staying overnight, other times not, but always rushing back to be in our gym by 2:30 the next day.

In the old days a basketball coach's season would end in March or April and he might not see his team until they came back in September. There was no summer school. The kids went home, got jobs, and came back for classes in the fall. Now we've made it so that we are recruiting, running camps, or seeing kids all summer long. It takes a toll on coaches and families.

The season is long and arduous and it takes a physical and mental toll. When it ends, I go with my wife, Ellen, to our house in Florida, just the two of us. I just dial it back. We walk the beach and exercise. I read and I think and I evaluate the previous season. I'll be on the phone some, talking to people, but not a lot. It's my time to recharge, because without that, I've learned, there's no way I can be what I have to be for my team and these kids. I need it in order to build back the fight, the energy, and the will.

If you walked into our practice gym, the voice you would mostly hear is mine. I've got the chart in my hands or on a table at half-court that says what we're going to do. I've got the whistle. That's how I want it because I think it's easier for players to be tuned to one voice rather than getting directions in surround sound, from all directions.

But the practice plan has the input of all the assistants because we've spent time together working on it. During practices, they are on the court running drills and making suggestions and corrections.

It's important for me to know what I'm not good at—or what I don't have time for—and throw that over to somebody else. Like I said, I want metrics but I'm certainly not going to keep the numbers myself and I'm not going to make the first pass at analyzing them. I count on Joel Justus to pass them on to me and say, "This is what I'm seeing. This is what I think they mean." My other assistants will have opinions as well. If I want to look more deeply at the numbers myself and form my own conclusions, I have them in front of me. But I trust them to do the analysis. We find out that a certain offensive set isn't working, and we talk about why and whether we can fix it or just run something else instead. If the numbers tell us something about a certain player, I might be the one to talk to him, but I'm just as likely to ask Kenny or one of the others to have that first conversation.

I also have each assistant do a scouting report of each team we are getting ready to play. The reason is that I know that they are studying tape and it makes me feel more comfortable when they are giving me suggestions on the bench that I know are well thought out and researched. I get the Ronald Reagan version of the reports—two pages so I can bang through it. If I need more, it's there for me. (And I also spend plenty of time myself watching game tape.)

Hiring assistant coaches in basketball has changed drastically over the last five years. I'm looking for certain things now that go well beyond the coaching of skills or the scouting of opponents. Can that person create relationships with our current players to bring them together? Can he be the individual workout guru who is on call twenty-four hours a day? Can he create relationships with recruits, their families, and their coaches? Does he have existing relationships that can put us in touch with the best players in the country?

Here is another important point about seats on the bus—and which one is my seat. In any organization, there are at least three time periods you are dealing with: the present, the near-term future, and the long-term future. I think it's really hard for a leader to be truly focused on all of those at once.

For us, during the season, the present is easy to define: It's the next game. Each practice session and film session is focused on that. There's a choreography to game day. We have a shootaround and a pregame meal. We do the same things no matter if it's early in our nonconference schedule, and we're playing a game that should not present a huge challenge—or we're in the Final Four. We don't change it up.

The near-term future is the next handful of games on the schedule. There's usually one upcoming that our fans are all excited about and ESPN is building up as some kind of "showdown."

The long-term future is just what it sounds like: the recruiting of next year's class of players and the class after that. Details about my fantasy basketball camp, which benefits my charitable foundation. Discussions, say, over improvements to Rupp Arena, where we play our home games.

I deal with the present: the next game. I've got the help of all my assistants but I'm still enough of a competitor that I've got my nose in there on everything because I want to win. I am deeply involved with the long-term future, because that is part of my role as, essentially, the CEO of Kentucky basketball. Where's this program going in the next year, two years, five years? I can't hand that over to one of my assistants.

The seat on the bus that I give up is the near-term future—those games coming around the corner. I don't want to hear about them or think about them. The reality, though, is that somebody has to.

I'll use an example from last year's schedule to explain how I deal with it. Early in the season we had games at home against Albany and the New Jersey Institute of Technology. They were on consecutive nights, a Friday and Saturday, which is very unusual—but we'd done it that way because we had Duke coming up that Tuesday in the United Center in Chicago.

Neither of these first two games was against a pushover. NJIT went into Ann Arbor, Michigan, the previous season and upset Michigan. Albany had made it into the NCAA tournament the last three seasons. Those are the teams I was focused on.

My assistants, though, had looked at game tape of Duke. They had to, with just a one-day turnaround and a plane trip before we played. They had talked about what they'd seen, and John Robic, who is the assistant most involved in preparing for upcoming opponents, had already drawn their offensive and defensive sets so we could replicate them on the practice floor.

When the NJIT game was over, I had Duke tape on my iPad. It had been downloaded by our video coordinator, Tim Asher. I looked at it that night. We went on to defeat Duke, 74–63.

The Importance of Nonnegotiables

To be fully empowered you have to first take full responsibility. You can't be someone who cuts corners when you think nobody is looking, and you can't look for places to hide. You have to stay in the tent with everyone else.

And it's not just a matter of following rules. What I'm talking about is making a true commitment to the program and each other. I can lay down the nonnegotiables, but what I want, ultimately, is for the players to hold themselves accountable.

The extreme depth of talent I lead allows me to be more demanding. There's no reason for any of my players to violate a nonnegotiable. If they do, they know I'll grab someone off the bench and sub them right out of the game.

In the course of games, I ask four simple things, all of them having to do with effort:

1. *Transition defense.* It will be a sin for us to give up a break-out basket. The only way we get outnumbered on our defensive side of the court is if they run harder than us. Most years, on defense, we are really hard to score against. There's no reason for us to give up fast-break points rather than making a team beat us five-on-five.

2. *Dive for loose balls.* Be the aggressor. When there's a loose ball on the floor, the guy who dives is the one who comes

up with it. If the player from the other team hits the floor and comes up with the ball, fine—but you'd better not be on your feet, looking at him. You've got to be down there with him in a wrestling match.

3. *Sprint the floor.* On offense and defense, after each made or missed basket, we don't jog. If you're tired, wave your hand at the bench and I'll bring somebody else in.

4. *No uncontested three-point shots.* A three-point shot in college basketball is anything beyond 20 feet, 9 inches, which is a shorter distance than in the NBA. For a competent outside shooter, it is not a difficult shot if you're standing out there all by yourself. In our game, it's the great equalizer. You could have a team with more talented players, but if you allow a team to stand out there wide open and make fifteen of them, you're almost always losing that game. That's why we stress defending it so much.

The pure math of the three-pointer can cost you games—and the momentum change if a team hits two or three of them in a row can take you right out of a contest. We absolutely refuse to give good shooters open threes. We "run them off" the three-point line and make them drive it into the heart of our defense, where we usually have shot blockers. They can take their chances with that, or pull up in the lane and take a jump shot or floater on the move. If you make a high percentage of those, you're an NBA player, and we face some of those. But the reality is, most college players will only make 20 to 28 percent of the shots we want to force them into, and that's a good percentage for us.

In practice and in other settings when we're together, I have another nonnegotiable. Earlier I mentioned giving kids a fist bump or a hug when they come into my office and when they leave. When we're doing drills, our kids have to touch as they walk off the court from a drill. If there are eight players coming off the court with you, you are touching all eight. It's a way for them to connect to each other. It takes the communication away from me and puts it onto them. It gets them away from thinking about themselves and to focus on their teammates instead.

The more you touch and the more you talk, the closer they get. This isn't bowling or golf. This is five of us playing off one another.

More than any other sport I'm aware of, basketball is a talking game—and by that I mean talking in the course of competition. If you have never had an opportunity to sit at courtside, you might not know it, but on successful teams, when players are on defense they are constantly calling out to each other. They'll warn each other when there's an offensive player setting a screen. Someone will call out "Switch!" if a defender can't get around a screen and stay with his man, or "I've got ball!" when the other team is fast-breaking and someone must step forward and guard the ball handler. A player who is beaten might simply shout "Help!"

High-powered, fast-moving companies often talk about "connected work environments." Everybody should be in the loop—copied on emails, included in key meetings. This is our form of connection. It's moment to moment. Physical.

It's not always easy to get young players to talk. They're too worried about themselves. But when teams are empowered there's a lot of it. There's talking, touching, hugging, smiling—all signs that the guys are into what they're doing together. Someone who knows basketball could walk into a gym blindfolded and just listen to a practice and get a good sense of the emotional connectedness of a team.

BEYOND THE ARC

- Coach your team. Distractions take you away from what you do best.
- All of your people, no matter their role or their status, should feel like they played an essential part in your organization's success.
- As a leader, find time to recharge your batteries. Take time to think, take time to exercise, take time to be away from the chaos of your business.
- Being empowered does not mean freedom from rules. All successful companies have their own set of nonnegotiables—firm principles that everyone knows and follows.
- When you lay down a set of high standards that everyone must follow—and ambitious goals they all agree on—it binds your people together. Even as empowered individuals, they are all marching together toward a common purpose.
- Communication connects the entire work environment. In our sport, the great teams have the best communication. Do you have a connected work environment?

What Were You Doing Before the Camera Focused on You?

In practices and games, you'll often hear me yell, "Two hands!" by which I mean that players must rebound the ball with two hands. It drives me crazy when a player just sticks out one hand to try to snag a rebound. The obvious downside is that he might not come up with it—or he gets the ball but someone is just going to grab it from him.

But there's another factor: The player who reaches with one hand probably has not done his work. He has not moved his feet to get himself in proper position, or he hasn't boxed out his opponent.

He's taken an easy way out, and therefore can't get both his paws on the ball. So when I yell, "Two hands!" what I'm really saying is, "Do this whole other set of things correctly."

"Play him before he catches the ball" is another frequent instruction from our staff, and it is also about preparation and habits. When you're watching basketball on TV at home and you see a player receive a pass on the wing and blow by his defender, you probably have not even seen the key part of the sequence.

What was the defender's posture before that guy caught the ball? Was he in what we call athletic position, with his butt down and his legs bent? That's a hard way to play for a whole defensive possession—as many as thirty seconds, following your man, fighting through traffic—and it's much easier to stand straight up and figure you'll spring into action when the guy makes his move. But it's too late by then.

Everybody seems to have energy for offense. You're scooting around, running sideline to sideline, hunting shots. You hit one or two and you're even more sprightly. I'm open! Pass it to me again! However, a great deal of the physical conditioning we do is designed for our players to have that same intensity on defense. The one-handed rebounder or defender who is not in proper position is often a tired player—or one who has not trained himself to push through physical discomfort.

And even on offense, there is an element of posture, positioning, and preparation that fans do not always notice. I tell my players, "Be ready to shoot." That means that they must be spring-loaded, athletically, before the ball touches their hands. The posture is the same as what we're seeking on defense.

Think of some of the NBA's great three-point shooters, past and present: Reggie Miller, Ray Allen, and Paul Pierce, or Steph Curry and Klay Thompson, the "Splash Brothers" of the current Golden State Warriors. You're admiring their shot, but the fact is, these guys are in unbelievable shape. They're wearing out the defenders chasing after them. And then when they do get an open look, they have the lift to elevate and release the ball in perfect form.

These things are no different from what goes into taking a final exam or making a sales presentation. If it doesn't go your way, sometimes it's because you didn't get the job done in the room. You made the wrong guess or the wrong move. But the greater likelihood is that you lost it before you got there because you didn't do your work beforehand.

Preparation is self-empowerment. I can't give that to you. You've got to earn it yourself.

BEYOND THE ARC

- Everything that we do in public, during our games, is preceded by hundreds of hours of practice. If you come up short at a key moment, in sports or business, look back very closely and critically at your preparation.
- Why did you fail to perform in the room? Did you have the wrong person making the presentation? Insufficient research? Did you rehearse for the big moment or just figure that everyone would know what to do and rise to the occasion?

You Don't Have to Make Them All, but You Can't Miss Them All

I tend to talk more about effort and habits than results, because that's what can always be controlled. But as much as I harp on preparation, there is a performance aspect to what we do. Whatever you do in practice—or on your own in the weight room, late at night shooting foul shots alone in the gym, or watching film—there does come a time when you must step into the spotlight.

The way I put it is: What are you going to do when the popcorn starts popping? When you walk into the arena, pull on the uniform, and see the stands start filling up and smell the scent of popcorn and hot dogs wafting down from the concession stands, how do you react?

I've had a few guys—Brandon Knight was one—who I didn't realize how good they were until we started playing games. Brandon was really good in practice. Hard worker. Focused. But when the popcorn popped, I was looking at something different. He seemed even quicker. He shot the ball better. That was just a gift of his, part of his mental makeup. He could get amped up for a game without losing any of his poise.

He wasn't alone in that. A lot of the extremely talented players I've coached feel, rightly, superior, and know they can impose their will in games. They have that swagger. But I've also seen guys that practice like crazy and are unbelievable in drills, and then they get in the game and can't do it.

I've been surprised at times because I expected something different. As a coach you can encourage them, but it has to come from within. The one thing I can't do is make them less accountable. My players are accountable for effort and practice habits, but I'm not ever going to tell them performance doesn't matter. Shooting—and especially foul shooting—is where it comes up most clearly.

To be quite honest, the act of making a foul shot is not one of the more difficult things in sports. It's not pole-vaulting 18 feet or hitting a 96-mile-per-hour fastball. A player with proper form—bends his knees, lets the ball go with his fingertips toward the front of the rim on his follow-through—should make most of them.

When he misses, he might be long or short, but he shouldn't be wide right or wide left.

I rarely have a player who cannot make at least 6 or 7 out of 10 foul shots in practice. Some players might make more. But these same kids, at times, will go out and miss all four of their foul shots in a game—or go 1 for 7 because the other team wants to keep putting them on the line. Their efforts keep getting worse. The first one spins out, the second hits the front rim, the third is sprayed so wide right that all it hits is the backboard.

It's ugly, and it has a demoralizing effect on our team. We had a good offensive trip down the floor and earned some points but now we've got someone on the foul line who's shooting it like he's wearing mittens.

I have to say to this player, "Look, you don't have to make all your foul shots, but if you're missing them all, that's an issue. We've got guys hitting them at 80 percent or better and I'm not asking you to do that. But with what you're doing right now, if it doesn't improve, I can't have you on the floor at the end of close games."

The truth is, I may not be able to play this guy that much at all, because what often happens is that the bad shooting undermines the rest of his game. He hesitates to be aggressive offensively because someone might foul him.

I don't talk about it a lot because that actually can make it worse, but I just make it clear: You've got to figure out a way to solve this. Get in the gym yourself, work through it mentally, because in most cases you are talking yourself either into something or out of something. In this case, they miss a shot or two and think, Oh, no, I'm going to miss the next one. At that point, they are always correct.

I wrote earlier about tracking statistics that show effort, and those are important because effort should lead to results. But it does not in every case, and we are a results-driven business—just like all businesses. That's why I have to let kids know that, at a certain point, you've got to make some of these shots. It's not complicated. If you don't, we're not going to win, so therefore I can't play you as much.

Good Players Make Hard Plays Look Easy, Bad Ones Make Easy Plays Look Hard

Another note on shooting and accountability: I wrote earlier in this chapter that everyone has a seat on the bus. Like every team in basketball, we've got players we count on to score from the outside. They might do other things, but that's their seat, and it's essential to have these guys.

It doesn't matter how good your inside players are: If you don't have kids who can score from the perimeter, you probably don't have an efficient offense. The defense packs it in and your big guys are wrestling with three guys just to get a shot off.

Now, every shooter goes through hot and cold streaks, and it's not unusual for even a great shooter to miss three, four, or five makeable shots in a row. Jamal Murray made 41 percent of his three-pointers for us last year, which is good; in conference play, the games later in the season after he had his feet on the ground, he shot better than 44 percent, which is really good.

In February, in a game against Tennessee, he shot 3 for 12 from beyond the arc. The next game he made 8 of the 10 three-pointers he put up against Florida. That's just the way it goes.

Jamal had the confidence to keep shooting.

There are other guys who respond differently. They lose confidence and pass up the shots. My rule is simple: If it's your shot, you'd better take it. I don't care how many you just missed. Your teammates worked to get you that shot; if you pass it, you're putting it back on their plates. I have very rarely taken shooters out of the game for missing shots. But I have, many times, subbed them out for not shooting.

Jamal was super-comfortable with the ball. He had big hands and really good control with his off hand. He could do all kinds of tricks. Flip it over his head from half-court and swish it (believe me, we have video of him doing it). Head the ball into the hoop, like a soccer player. If the Globetrotters came into our gym to scout, he would be the guy they would want.

We had to teach Jamal the difference between a winning play and a losing play—which is usually the same as the difference between an easy one and a hard one. Early in the season, he would pass up an open shot, dribble into traffic, and try to spin the ball off the backboard with his left hand. He would tell me, "But Coach, I can make that shot." He didn't quite understand that he could get a better shot—a more efficient shot. Early in the shot clock, he'd jack up a difficult three-point attempt rather than run the actions that would get him an easier one.

These things were the source of my tug-of-war with Jamal. He ended the season averaging 20 points a game, the highest of any player during my Kentucky tenure and of any player I've ever coached since Dajuan Wagner, in 2002 at Memphis. He came close to breaking Steph Curry's NCAA single-season three-point record for a freshman, and his scoring really picked up in the season's second half—at the same time he was actually taking fewer shots. The best players I've coached made the hardest plays look simple. Most freshmen make easy plays look hard.

BEYOND THE ARC

- Young talent will often make the easy tasks look difficult. Those who are more seasoned make the hard things look easy, and you must move younger people in that direction.
- Courage is essential. You must have people who are willing to take the lead at big moments, even if that means occasional failure.

Empowered Teams Have Servant Leaders

Even as I am still recruiting them, I will talk to players about the concept of servant leadership. It sounds vaguely religious but it is not. The concept comes from the late Robert Greenleaf, an executive for AT&T who in 1970 wrote an essay titled "The Servant as Leader"—which defines a leader as someone who measures his own success by the success achieved by those around him. He argued that the people within an organization are the organization; if the leader cares first for them, looking after their well-being and helping them reach their goals, then the whole enterprise will thrive.

Basketball teams are delicately balanced in terms of the personalities involved and the emotions at play. We only have a dozen or so players, all of them talented and ambitious. There are always some natural leaders among them, and some followers. Sometimes you have a player who sees himself as a leader but is not as equipped in that area as he assumes. (Maybe he's always been the biggest and the best and others have just followed, but it takes a lot more than that.)

Greenleaf did not believe that leading was something that just one person did. It wasn't top-down. He wrote that each individual has it within himself to be a servant leader—to pull others up along with him even as he is striving toward his own goals.

All of my successful teams have strong leaders among the players—and, in fact, they have multiple leaders. There comes a point in seasons when I can almost feel a shift—where I recede some and the most powerful force leading the team is the collective will of my players and the love and commitment they feel for each other. They are truly playing for each other.

In February 2016, I was given two technical fouls by an official and was ejected from our game at South Carolina. We had not even played three minutes, meaning we had thirty-seven minutes left to play as I was escorted back to our locker room. The Game-cocks' home arena in Columbia was bad luck for me; I had also been kicked out of our game there in 2014. Some people wrote that I had wanted to be tossed this time, on the theory that it would energize my team, but I would never do that. It would be totally unprofessional. When the players came in at halftime, I apologized to them for losing my composure.

But there was a benefit to what occurred. We played perhaps our best game of the season, blowing out a tough team on their home court, 89–62. I had never been more proud of a team. I told the media when we got back to Lexington, "The best part of that last game is I could step away—didn't do it on purpose—but I could step away and see that this team was empowered. They were running and doing the things that we had taught and they didn't need me there. It's not me driving them anymore. It's not me battling them anymore. I don't need to. They're dragging us now, and that's what I try to do every year."

Some people even tried to say after that game that the team was better without me on the bench, and that didn't bother me. I figured if that's what they think, then I've done my job.

Kenny Payne, who had taken over for me on the bench, told the writers that he had not called any offensive plays. He tended to the defense, and Tyler Ulis, our sophomore point guard, ran the offense. "Every now and then I may have interjected something, but at the end of the day it was his show," he said. That might have been a little overstated—Kenny called out some offenses—but I had already stated in the weeks before that Tyler was functioning almost like an assistant coach and running the team on the floor.

It's unusual to have one kid be that strong a leader, but that's what we had. One important lesson is that it did not get in the way of other players being leaders. Just as I try to model leadership for Tyler, he was modeling it for his teammates. They were becoming servant leaders.

Jamal Murray was a leader on that team, stepping up at big moments in big games. Alex Poythress, in his own strong and quiet way, showed leadership, as did Marcus Lee.

They were all feeding off Tyler's confidence.

One thing I did have to sometimes monitor with Tyler—as with any player who emerges as a strong leader—is that his teammates were not putting too much on him. As the coach, I want to throw off some of my power and give it to the team. But it can't just fall on one guy.

I said that to the team: Tyler is playing a lot of minutes, he's playing ninety feet of full-court defense, and he's got the ball in his hands a lot. He's got the courage to take big shots but he can't be the only one.

If he sets you up for a shot, and it's your shot, you'd better take it. If you pass it back to him, I'll take you right out of the game and you might sit there for a while.

I couldn't possibly create a leader like Tyler Ulis, but with a kid like that, I do have to guide him. The art of coaching extreme talent includes coaching talent of all kinds—including extreme leadership talent. He was not my peer or truly an assistant coach, though at times it was easy to forget that. The fact is that he was still a teenager, nineteen years old until January of his second and final season with us. The previous season, after his freshman year, one NBA team was said to have asked all our kids at the NBA combine which of their teammates they would pick to go to war with. Every one of them gave the same answer: Tyler.

The first thing about having a player like that is I have to have my own confidence, as does the rest of my staff. I think there are some coaches, especially younger ones, who might be afraid to have a kid that strong. We had a group of elite players, but he had a total grip on the team.

As the coach, you have an unbelievable relationship with that guy. You have to understand that when he's among his teammates, in private, and they're complaining about me—"he's too hard on us; we need a day off"—he might be in there agreeing with them. I don't want him to be viewed as someone who just kisses the coach's butt. But I also believe there's a point where he would be like, look, this is what we have to do, and he's not representing their point of view, or my point of view, but his own. And it will be a sensible position based on what we need to do to win.

There came a time when I told Tyler that I actually wanted more leadership from him—or, more specifically, that I wanted it to extend off the court. Our kids live together. They eat together.

They're together a lot. Tyler would sometimes go his own way, or go off with one teammate. Everybody needs his or her own time. I know I do. But I worried that with Tyler, the balance was off.

I said to him, "You're the best floor general I've ever coached. You're not as good a leader off the court, though." He said, "What do you mean?" I replied, "You're not around the guys as much as they want. What you do on the court is not enough. They look up to you. They need you around more. But you can't lead them on the court if you don't lead them off of it."

That's where mentorship comes in. Are your leaders also serving as mentors? Are they invested in others' success? Getting my leaders to lead off the court puts them in a position to bring teams even closer together. They have to know you've got their back.

You also have to do things the right way. My guys can't take shortcuts in the classroom, miss curfew, or show up late at meetings and then lead. That leadership is hollow and the guys see right through it.

It's the same way in any other facet of life. You can't take shortcuts and then demand excellence with others. It doesn't work. Leadership and empowerment are really about a will to win. What will you do to make sure that happens? Tyler cared so much that he would cry after losses. He wasn't the only one. He refined his skills and his decision-making every single week he was in our program, so that he knew he could read defenses and respond. If they let him have his offense, he would score 25 points. If they collapsed and took it away, he would put up 11 or 12 assists.

Tyler grew up pretty tough in Chicago. He had his own goals. But the beauty of it was, his teammates knew that Tyler's heart beat for all of them. The only way he knew to play basketball was when everyone's dreams were wrapped up together.

BEYOND THE ARC

- Servant leadership starts at the top. Mentorship is a form of servant leadership.
- Mentorship is no-cost or low-cost with a high reward. It is a combination of continuing education, on-the-job training, and team bonding.
- Does your organization create mentors organically? Do you have people who just step up and take that role?
- If not, do you need to create a more formal mentoring structure in order to make sure you are fully benefiting from the wisdom and knowledge that can be seeded throughout your workplace?
- Have you properly mentored people who can assume your duties? What does your organization look like if you are gone for a week? Do you fear the wheels will come off? An empowered workforce should be able to operate smoothly for a period of time without its leader.

9

MAKE IT ABOUT SOMETHING BIGGER

On non–game days, I dress for work in sneakers and athletic clothes and teach guys to put a ball through a hoop more than the other team. However, if that were all there was to it, I don't think I would still be at it—or at least I hope not. But I consider myself an educator as well as a coach. My students are young men who are going to engage with a world beyond the confines of a basketball court. I try my best to guide them in a way that will benefit themselves and others—and to steer them away from behaviors that could damage their futures.

One of the first things I'm concerned about is the fact that they are public figures—in most cases, before they have hit a stage of development that really equips them to handle it. They have matched their unusual size and physical grace with an ability to set a goal and work toward it, meaning they've spent thousands of hours in gyms dribbling, passing, and shooting basketballs. Extreme talent, however, in any field, does not necessarily equate with extreme wisdom or extreme judgment. Part of my job is to widen their worldview, because it's good for them—and also protective.

It's one reason I ask them their "why." I had a player named Julius Mays for just one year. He was a senior graduate transfer, and his answer to my question was, "I'm my mother's only son and I refuse to fail." Others have talked about making a difference in their communities, or the country they come from. For some there is almost a desperation driving them. They can't give up. They must push on.

In my program, I want to help instill a wider view of the world, something beyond the game itself that gets them up in the morning, drives them into the gym, and makes them not want to let go of the rope. We all love basketball, but if they walk away from me and that's all they know or care about, I haven't done my job.

If It's Predictable, It's Preventable

Because they are under a public microscope, as successful people often are, what happens out in the real world can derail their lives, not just their basketball careers, and they must hear that from me in very direct language. On New Year's Day of 2016, I talked to my team about relationships and sex. It was a version of what I've been advising teams in the years since there has been more attention and sensitivity to issues relating to gender and violence on college campuses.

"You've got to be disciplined in your relationships," I told them. "Pay attention to what's happening on campuses. If a woman says no, that means no. If a woman strikes you, you run. You put your hands in your pockets and you run. If she hits you over the head with a bottle, you run. Standing six foot ten in front of a judge, next to five foot four, you're going to jail."

I know this is not the easiest advice to hear or take. Eighteen or nineteen years old is not an age of great self-control. What I'm saying is that my players could be in a situation where they feel they are in the right—and may in fact be right—but it won't matter. Their status and future prospects are such that in any confrontation or misunderstanding, they likely will have more to lose than the other person. If it's a judgment call, they may lose. That's something they have to understand.

There are some coaches who discourage players from having girlfriends. They think it takes up too much time or separates them from the group. I understand how that can happen—and in some cases, it has hurt guys—but it's not my place to try to get in the way of it. Part of life is learning how to be with another person. If they're attracted to someone, I can't say, "Hey, can you just put that on hold until you're done playing basketball for Kentucky?" Then what happens if they leave here and go to the NBA and they're in that whole scene, and it's all new to them? That's its own kind of danger.

I wrote in an earlier chapter about the past being the past. Well, in terms of social interactions on campus, we are not in the 1970s anymore, and they have to know that.

I don't try to put them in some kind of lockdown but I do sometimes have a curfew, usually midnight, a little later on weekends (though not the night before a game). It's just a feel or an instinct thing, rather than the fact that somebody got in trouble.

I love every one of them and care about them. They have dreams they want to fulfill. I want to take them out of any situations that could mess that up. Guys can go over to the gym at two in the morning to work on their game if they've got extra energy. They can grab someone and go get shots up. That's a good way to spend time.

Lexington is a pretty quiet city for a college town, but like anywhere else, there are places you could find trouble. I don't want my players in any clubs, here or back home. They're recognizable. I tell them that if they want attention, go to the mall. People will want to take pictures with you. Go to the movies. Stay in the lobby before it starts, hang out, have a Coke. I'm not kidding. You'll get loved that way. Fame is new to them. Some may want that experience. Or if you really want love, get a dog.

To be a coach is, admittedly, to be a little paranoid about what's coming around the corner and what could happen. We've always got an important game coming up, and as we get into the season, the tournament looms. I want them all safe, sound, healthy, eligible to play. If you've raised teenagers, think of the feeling in the pit of your stomach when they go out at night—and your relief when they walk back in the door. Well, I have fifteen of them.

We talk about a lot of things that can trip them up, some of them broader issues, like complacency. If a kid is doing well, I will say: "Okay, what can you add to your game? What's next?" A feeling of satisfaction can stop a kid just as surely as a mistake can. The same goes for the team as a whole.

What I call the "clutter"—the noise in the press, social media, or from back home—is another frequent topic of conversation. There are always going to be people trying to create divisions—telling my kids I should sit one of their teammates and play them more; that I'm playing them out of position; that the offense we're playing does not properly "suit their game." It's inevitable. All they've got to do is look and they can find it.

I have to be real with my players and let them know that some of these people have an opinion they just want to express—and some others are probably in it for their own personal gain. They want to get into your inner circle because they think there's money in it for them down the road. They're telling you what they think you want to hear, rather than what you need to hear, and you just can't listen. It's the worst kind of clutter and you've got to block it out.

Have I mentioned I worry about everything? Well, at some point during the season I'm sure to tell them that the flu is going around and to make sure to frequently wash their hands.

Dealing with Social Media

Social media is now part of everyday life. You can hate it if you want but it's not going away. My job is to educate my players. In terms of social media, I want them to use it to create their own brand— and not do anything to sully it. Like all other young people, they have to understand that whatever they post or retweet is up there forever. The difference for them, as opposed to normal kids their age, is that it will be noticed.

I ask them, How do you want to be seen? What impression do you want to leave in the public's mind? Because whatever you put out there, that's who people are going to think you are, and it's very difficult to change that impression if you've done something regrettable.

I read a story recently that said some NBA players check their phones in the locker room during halftime of games. Even if they're not technically supposed to, they reach into their lockers and sneak a quick look.

I wouldn't allow that on my team, but I'm not naive about the role social media plays in the lives of my players. Like just about every other person their age, they exist in two places at once—

where they are, physically, at any given moment; and the virtual world they are looking at on their phones. They are constantly checking Twitter, Snapchat, Facebook, Instagram, and I assume other sites I haven't even heard of yet.

I am on social media and I use it a lot, especially Twitter. I have found it useful in putting out what I want to say without it being filtered through traditional media. If they've got bias, I can just bypass it. I post but I never respond to other tweets, nor do I read them. For me, social media is a one-way communication tool because I don't want to get caught up in the clutter. I have people who send out what I want on my social media feeds (I wouldn't even know how to do it) and then filter back what the response is if I ask. Other that that, I don't want to see it. I give my players the same advice. Don't respond to individual people on social media, even if it's criticism. They're in a position where it's safest not to have a two-way conversation, except on private channels with friends. In public, put out what you have to say and leave it at that.

If I'm tweeting in response to some controversy, or anything that has me worked up, I make sure, as I said earlier, that there are three or four sets of eyeballs on whatever I'm putting out, because I can get emotional. I'm Italian, so sometimes whatever I'm feeling in my gut is something I want to immediately express. It's just who I am, and I need people to slow me down and make sure I don't say anything stupid. I'll show my proposed tweets to people I trust—usually including Eric Lindsey, who oversees our media relations and social media efforts; and Metz Camfield, who runs my website—and they'll often say, "Why don't you hold off on this, Cal?" or "Why don't we say something like this instead?" I listen to them. I don't argue.

I advise my players not to get caught up in all the basketball stuff on social media, especially who's up and who's down on the

NBA draft boards. It's distracting, inaccurate, and ultimately poisonous to them if they really start swimming in it. But their futures are so tied to a lot of the stuff being written about them that I think it's difficult for some of them not to look.

I think we've been more successful in teaching them not to tweet or retweet things they will regret. It's something young people do at times. My own son and daughters have done it. I'll say, "Why did you retweet that? Basically, you're saying the same stupid thing that person just put out there."

I'm never going to tell my players not to be on social media. But we've been pretty good at teaching them to use it smartly and to take care about what they write. (We do have people who look at their accounts just in case they slip up.)

My concern, as always, is for their long-term futures. If you tweet something you regret, it can go viral and stay out there, and no matter what else you do on the basketball court or elsewhere, you're known as the dope who made a comment that was viewed as sexist or racist or homophobic or whatever. We tell our guys, Look, this is stuff that can affect your future and your brand. Even if what you've put out there was misunderstood and doesn't represent who you are, it can hurt you.

Having said all that, I am a fan of social media, a big proponent. It's a tool, and it can be incredibly useful—but just like any tool, it can also be dangerous. We have rules for our players and points of emphasis regarding social media, but we don't discourage them from using it. Just the opposite. I want them to embrace it and learn to use it smartly.

- Play war games with your staff. It it's predictable, it's preventable. Talk about scenarios before they happen.
- Does your organization have a policy on use of social media? Do you educate your people about it?
- Talented people tend to be early adopters who want to have a public profile. Whatever the new platform is, they are likely to be on it. Teach them to use it as a tool for good, rather than something that hurts them or your company.

Cultivating Curious Minds

Social media has changed everything that we do, how we think, how we learn, what we see and listen to. Just on that basis alone, I have to know about it and be fluent in it. But one way in which I'm still old-fashioned is that I still do most of my learning from reading—mostly books.

I'm not usually reading for the sake of being moved emotionally. I don't read novels. I read books by people who know something about leadership, psychology, or coaching—Harvey Mackay, Simon Sinek, Ken Blanchard, Jon Gorden, John Maxwell, Bob Rotella, Pat Riley, Mike Tomlin, Marvin Lewis, and dozens of others—so I can get ideas and help these guys on my team.

I feel that if my players are readers, they'll be lifelong learners, and I frequently give them books. When Willie Cauley-Stein was here, he told me during his freshman season that he did not like school. But it turned out that he did not like to read. We started our own private book club together, reading books such as *The*

Energy Bus. This helped encourage him, and even though he left after his junior year, he is now close to earning a degree.

One thing that many fans don't understand is that it takes a lively mind to excel in sports—just about any sport. My elite players are always curious. They're the ones reading the books and looking at extra tape. If I bring my friend Bob Rotella, a sports psychologist, in for a visit, they want to talk to him. Just like they will spend extra time adding an offensive move, they want to find out if he has anything that will enhance their mental approach.

Their curiosity and inclination to want to see the bigger picture translate into how they play. They don't have blinders on. They see a court with nine other players. You don't have to stop practice and say, "Did you see what was going on over there?" They saw it. If they didn't make the right pass at that moment, they will the next time.

Even my brightest and most curious players are usually not very aware of what's going on in the world. That's because of their age, and probably their generation. I doubt that many of them grew up with daily newspapers being thrown onto their front step, with that becoming a thing of the past. If they have any knowledge of current events, it's probably from whatever headlines they're grabbing from Facebook.

But some of the stuff happening in the world is coming at them, and I think it's important to make them aware of it. After Michael Brown, the young man from Ferguson, Missouri, was shot and killed by a police officer, the controversy over that incident and some others like it became a topic on college campuses. Players on the Missouri football team became actively involved and athletes elsewhere were taking stands and making statements.

I thought it was something we should talk about, because my players might one day want to become involved—or, because of their high profiles, people might want to draw them in. One day before practice, in the room where we usually watch film and draw the upcoming opponent's plays on a whiteboard, we talked about it. My main point was that whatever they did or did not do, it should be based on knowledge.

"Never let anybody use you because of who you are," I said. "If you're going to stand in front of the line, know why you're up there. Research it. Do you want to be involved or not? Why do you want to be involved? How can you effect change? Can you effect change for the good? If so, then you always do it."

My sense was that my players were aware of these issues but not that deeply engaged. But this stuff was bubbling up. I wasn't worried about them becoming involved, or opposed to it. What we were going through, really, was the same thing we would do on the practice floor—this is what we may see; how are we going to deal with it? Just like in a game, I wanted them to be prepared and empowered.

I let them know that there are always consequences to taking social action. Not bad ones, necessarily, but they should always think about that, as well. You've taken a certain kind of step, and people may look at you differently. If you're calling on something to be boycotted, or if you are deciding to stay out of school or a practice or a game, there could always be consequences to that. They have to decide if that is worth it to them.

I took the opportunity to talk to them about how they should respond if they have their own interactions with police. "I'm going to throw this at you just because we're talking about this stuff," I said. "Policeman stops you, okay? You pull over. You roll down your window, and you put both hands on the steering wheel. Why do you do that? Why do you let him see both hands?"

Everybody answered in unison: "So the officer sees that you are not armed."

"Right," I said. "You turn the music down. Don't turn it up. Don't get out of the car."

I'm sure their own mothers had told them the same thing, probably repeatedly. But when they are with me on campus, I feel responsible. It's my job to teach them, and to the extent I can, to protect them.

The same would go for any leader who has talented young people under him. They are totally committed to your organization but they have lives outside work and connections to the wider world. I think you've got to be there with them, concerned about their futures and their fears. If you have an opportunity to help guide them, you should.

When It's Time to Let Go

I fully understand the good intentions of people who say kids should stay in school. Four years on a college campus is life-changing academically and socially. In terms of the basketball, I get the nostalgia. When I see a team of upperclassmen advance far into the NCAA tournament, or even win it, I admire the seamless teamwork that sometimes only comes from players who have been together for multiple seasons. If you love basketball, there's a beauty in that. (I know that the "Basketball Bennys," as I sometimes jokingly refer to the writers who cover our team, love it.)

But just like in Silicon Valley—where, as I wrote in Chapter 1, hotshot prospects are expected to change jobs frequently—staying in school too long usually does not benefit the career of an elite college basketball player. In the modern economy, no one can hoard talent. In *Superbosses*, the author Sydney Finkelstein writes that "when the time is right," a confident CEO "often encourages star talent to leave." After they move on, he continues, they become members of the boss's "strategic network in the industry," which is a good example of my former players who are now in the NBA. They become ambassadors of our program, as well as mentors to current players. A leader's role, generally, is to recruit talent, nurture it, and be realistic about the fact that it's going to move on sooner rather than later. In my business, it just moves on a little more quickly. The NBA may complain that most of the freshmen jumping into the league are too inexperienced to really contribute, but the fact is that NBA teams draft on potential. It's a futures market. They want the eighteen- and nineteen-year-olds, even if they sit on the bench for a year or get shipped out to the NBA Development League, known as the "D league," for further seasoning.

They'll never say it straight out but the league has a bias against players who stay in college. The fact is, the clock is ticking the moment a player arrives on campus. The evidence couldn't be more clear. A kid still in college at twenty-two years old has a diminished draft value. In the June 2015 draft, nine of the first fourteen players chosen (the "lottery" picks) were college freshmen and one was a sophomore. Two international players were selected, both of them teenagers. One junior (our own Willie Cauley-Stein) and one senior (Wisconsin's Frank Kaminsky) rounded out the lottery picks. In 2016, the first three players chosen were freshmen. Seven out of the first ten were teenagers.

Nearly every recent draft has been tilted in the same direction: toward youth, meaning predominantly college freshmen and teenagers from overseas. With an older college player, NBA executives believe they are looking at a more developed prospect. If he's been dominant against NCAA competition, they figure that's what he should be doing because he's got more experience and a more mature physique. He's got to be that much better than a younger prospect—but even if he is, his age may still be held against him. It's unfair but that's the way it is. This line of thinking surely affected Alex Poythress, who by his senior year with us was way better than he was as a freshman, but whose draft prospects were probably hurt by his staying that long.

The most recent draft was in some cases a little kinder to older players. For most of the 2015–16 season, the speculation was that Buddy Hield, a fearless, long-range shooting Oklahoma senior, would probably only be drafted somewhere in the middle or even toward the end of the draft's first round. It didn't matter that he was the best player on the court just about every night in one of the best conferences in college basketball. It didn't matter how many last-second game-winners he hit. At twenty-two, he was on the old side.

It took some ridiculous heroics on his part—46 points in a game against Kansas, 37 points in an Elite Eight victory over Oregon, a three-point shooting record on the season of 46 percent—to be considered a premier pick. And even then, he still just went sixth in the draft. I will never push one of my Kentucky players out the door, but I have to tell them at a certain point: You've shown the NBA your upside. You're a first-round draft pick. I love you—and I'd love to keep coaching you—but your time has come. If you're a lottery pick and want to come back, give me the reason why. The ones who would have been first-round picks and stayed have done so with a particular goal in mind, and it's worked out for them—Patrick Patterson, for example, wanted to get his degree and also work on his perimeter game and three-point shooting.

For these players, it's a business decision. When it comes time for them to make it, I can't worry about my own interests, the interests of college basketball, or even those of the Kentucky basketball program. I have to fulfill the solemn promise I made to the players' families when I accepted them on to my team: Your child comes first. I'll coach my team during the season, but the day it ends, it becomes solely about the futures of the individual players.

Every year, I've got as many as a half-dozen players who have to seriously consider leaving for the NBA. For some, the guys who are guaranteed lottery picks and instant millionaires, it's hardly even a choice. If they stay, they might get hurt or in some other way diminish their draft value.

For others, it can be more complicated. Skal Labissière was a good recent example, and a demonstration of how the NBA thinks. Skal was a little bit on the old side for a college freshman. If he had come back another year, he would have turned twenty-one during his sophomore year. I knew he was likely to want to go into the NBA draft, and that his family could use the help his contract would provide. Players must also be aware of who else is in the draft; the strength of the 2017 class, nationally, may not have benefited Skal. As crazy as it may seem, he could have come back to school, gotten way better, and actually dropped in the draft because he would have been one year older and because the next draft class could have been stronger. I don't always like it, but it's the way it is right now.

His late-season improvement was all the NBA needed to see. They still loved his potential. As one college basketball writer explained it, "NBA franchises remain more intrigued with Labissière's skill set and upside than they are concerned with his lack of production at the collegiate level."

I did not create that mind-set of NBA executives. But I have to be aware of it. How could I in good conscience push Skal to take a chance and come back and pass up the money? I couldn't because there were no guarantees he would improve his position, and the fact is, there is always the chance he could have made it worse. In the June 2016 draft, he was the twenty-eighth player chosen, by the Sacramento Kings (via the Phoenix Suns).

Even if he takes a little time to get acclimated, I would be very surprised if Skal does not ultimately have a long and successful pro career. There's too much extreme talent inside him for that not to happen.

Tyler Ulis also had somewhat of a decision to make. He developed into the best player on our 2015–16 team and the top college point guard in America, averaging 17 points a game and 7 assists with an extraordinary 3.6-to-1 assist-to-turnover ratio. He could have come back for his junior year, but it's hard to imagine he could have played any better or accomplished more.

He was already player of the year in the SEC and a consensus first-team all-American. He had only one drawback, and it wasn't something he could change: At five foot nine, he was at least five inches shorter than a typical NBA point guard. Because of that, there were NBA teams that wouldn't expend a high draft pick on him.

When I talked to Tyler about his decision, I told him that if he stayed another year at Kentucky, he might be able to show the NBA something new about his game. His three-point shooting percentage would probably improve some, since an elbow injury that plagued him through at least half the season had bothered his shooting stroke. Maybe he could rack up even more assists. Fewer turnovers. But he was still going to be five foot nine. And he, too, had to be aware of the next draft class. There was always the chance that Tyler could have had an even better season if he stayed but still not have improved his draft position.

Again, there would be NBA teams that wouldn't want him because of his size, but he didn't need every team to fall in love with him—he just needed one team with a high pick to select him. It was typical of the conversations I have every year. They're straightforward; they don't go on for hours or days. I just tell them: You can stay here if you want but if you think it's time to chase your dreams, I understand that and fully support your decision.

Tyler got drafted with one of the first picks in the second round, falling out of the first round for one reason only—his size. It was one thing for teams to see him on the court. When he walked into their offices and they were with him face-to-face, they couldn't get past the fact that not only was he five foot nine but he was also just 149 pounds.

The Suns, however, knew better. They signed him to a guaranteed contract with money that was the equivalent of what late-first-round picks get. Tyler played in the summer league with other NBA rookies, and by every account was one of the top two players—better than nearly every one of the lottery picks. It would be one of the safest bets you could make that he's going to have a long and productive professional career. The best part for our program is that he becomes another ambassador in the NBA for our program and our culture.

Measurable Results in the NBA

Measuring the results of our players in the NBA—all forty-one of them—is important to our ongoing recruiting. Their success rate is a very powerful tool when we talk to young people who have the same aspirations.

It is one thing to get drafted by the NBA and another to have a real career. Plenty of first-round picks wash out of the league quickly. They don't have the right skills or the proper maturity. They may get a rookie contract that guarantees them several million dollars, but if they do not deal with that windfall wisely—and don't get a second contract—they're probably not set for life. Basketball is over, or they're knocking around as hoops vagabonds in Europe or Asia, just trying to stay afloat.

By many different measures, our players have thrived—and I believe it's because we prepare them for success. There's a widely accepted statistic called Player Efficiency Rating (PER), which measures a variety of contributions. In the 2015–16 NBA season, 4 of the top 14 in the PER rankings had played for me at Kentucky—Anthony Davis, Enes Kanter, DeMarcus Cousins, and Karl-Anthony Towns. *Sports Illustrated* puts out a list of the top 25 NBA players under 25 years old, and on the 2015 list, three of the top four were ours (and 6 total in the list of 25). The total value of NBA contracts of players who have come through our program is more than $1 billion, and that doesn't include endorsements.

Most of these players were with us for just one season. If you look back at their last ranking before they came to our program—how they were rated against other high school seniors—I think it's fair to say they improved themselves dramatically. Eric Bledsoe was not widely considered a player who would go right to the NBA, but he did and quickly succeeded. Everybody thought highly of Karl, but some "experts" also considered him a little limited athletically. Another college player came in ranked higher. Karl is now routinely described as the league's next superstar.

Devin Booker was not even in the top tier of high school players, or one likely to be drafted after a season of college ball. But he was picked thirteenth in the NBA draft and then named to the NBA's first-team all-rookie squad—along with Karl-Anthony Towns. (Willie Cauley-Stein was selected to the second five.) As you can see, measuring the results will be a powerful tool as we go to recruit our next wave of extreme talent.

Being About Other People

I've never felt that the pursuit of money is the ultimate goal. But keep in mind that many of these kids came from impoverished families. Those contracts have changed the fortunes of those families, for generations to come. And they have helped change other people's lives, too, because our former players have given generously back to the communities where they were raised.

At the end of this past season, Anthony Davis and John Wall were named as two of the ten finalists for the NBA's Community Assist Award. Anthony's charitable foundation focuses on helping children and aiding the Boys and Girls Clubs in his native Chicago and in New Orleans, where he plays for the Pelicans. He has also aided in coastal restoration projects in Louisiana. John has given his time and money to a range of projects in Raleigh, North Carolina, where he was raised, and in Washington, DC, where he plays for the Wizards. He gave $400,000 to a nonprofit organization providing shelter, education, and meals to homeless children and their families, called DC's Bright Beginnings. At just twenty-five years old, John was selected as the winner of the award—the NBA's highest honor for community service. These are just two examples of the many players who have left with a social conscience and a determination to really make a difference.

When John and DeMarcus Cousins received their new max contracts a couple of years ago, the first thing both of them did was donate $1 million to charity.

I've said that one of my goals is to have twelve players in the NBA all-star game, and I think it's possible. But as the former coach of these young men, it is these charitable efforts that make me prouder than anything they could possibly do on a basketball court. I believe that just about every one of my players has used his money to do good, and do it generously.

As surely as we train to break a full-court press or run our dribble-drive offense, we condition our players to care about the world around them. I can't imagine doing it any other way. At Christmastime, we are in the neighborhoods of Lexington, distributing gifts to needy families. We visit sick children in hospitals, and some of our kids, without me even knowing, follow up and return on their own. When our team traveled to the Bahamas in the summer of 2014, we participated in a program called Samaritan's Feet and distributed new shoes. Karl-Anthony Towns came upon a young boy without socks and, with us having run out of socks to distribute, took his own off and gave them to the child. Our players have participated in a Hoops for Haiti telethon and one after the devastating Hurricane Sandy, along the East Coast. This past summer we participated in a Starkey Foundation Hearing mission where our players helped fit hearing aids for more than one hundred Kentucky residents. It is all part of what we do, and I hope that after my players are with us for a while, it will feel as natural as having a basketball in their hands on the practice court. I want that sense of charity and connectedness to the world to be in them, internalized as part of their identity, and I believe for almost every one of them, we have succeeded at that. They come to me as great kids and they leave as even better young men.

The title of this book, *Success Is the Only Option,* should be understood to define success in broad terms. If my players' lives are devoted exclusively to the pursuit of basketball stardom and money, I don't think they are fully embracing their blessings. And it would mean I have not done right by them.

My goal as their coach is for them to become the best version of themselves on the basketball court, and off it—as people who engage fully with the world and try to make a difference. Many of them have that opportunity, because they go on to fame and money. My greatest joy is to see them spread their success to their families, loved ones, and communities.

- Do you share your own curiosities with your people? Do your employees know that it's okay to talk about issues outside the workplace? What system do you have in place for people to talk about issues or curiosities outside the workplace?
- If you've read a good book, do you give them copies of it? I find it a good way to have an ongoing conversation even if it is not directly related to the work we are doing together.
- Encourage your employees to bond outside the workplace. Organize a happy hour. Take them all bowling. You all have a common objective, but it's important to have a life outside the job and present opportunities to discuss things outside the workplace. It makes for healthier work relationships and a better work environment. It shows you care.
- When your best people move up and on, do they become ambassadors for your business? Have you measured the success of those who have trained under you in other areas?

My Purpose

I've spent the last thirty years at the center of the storm—starting a coaching career at a young age, trying to figure out how to coach, how to be a good husband, how to be a good father, how to truly lead, how to motivate, how to bring people together. I am always focused on my "why." I always want to be sure that my own goals are big enough and wide enough.

I've gone from the business of basketball to the business of helping families. When we make our lives about others, life becomes easier. There's no doubt in my mind that it becomes more rewarding. What drives me now is making sure every one of the people who "work for me" is on a path of success. The true statement isn't that they work for me; I work for them. Their success is what brings joy and fulfills my life mission.

As for my players, I want them all to reach their dreams, to grow as men, to develop a socially minded mentality, to have a servant's heart and a curious mind, and to be the best version of themselves on and off the court. Some will become all-stars, MVPs, world champions, and gold medal winners. But if they become the best version of themselves, they can have peace of mind knowing that they've done their best. That is my hope for all of those whom I've come to lead.

Yes, I want to attend an NBA all-star game where twelve of the players in the game have played for me, and I believe it will happen. The challenge for all my players is to continue to grow, continue to learn, and continue to push toward being the best version of themselves.

I've been blessed to be put in this position. My grandparents were immigrants. My parents were high school graduates who had hopes and dreams that their children, through education and hard work, could make a difference, which is why I never take lightly this position I hold.

There is more than just one way to be a leader, but what I have tried to do in this book is to lay out a philosophy that I believe translates beyond basketball and applies to any person who is in the business of leading an organization and nurturing talent. I don't believe that team goals and individual goals are ever in conflict.

We create successful teams by binding our players to one another, to a common mission, and to the principles of shared sacrifice and servant leadership. I can't hold on to players forever. My goal, and one I believe we've been successful in achieving, is to set their sights ever higher and then send them off into the world with the skills, confidence, and poise they will need to succeed in their careers— and as human beings who contribute to the greater good. It is my mission in life, and one that I consider both a heavy responsibility and a tremendous privilege.

AFTERWORD

I know that readers will take their own lessons from this book—whichever chapters and passages have particular relevance to their lives and careers. I have written *Success Is the Only Option* for people striving to improve their performance as leaders, just as I am always striving to get better so I can lead our team to championships and help the young men I coach reach their dreams.

When I look back on the pages you've just read, several points stand out to me that will continue to be at the core of my leadership philosophy:

Recruit extreme talent and don't ever settle for people with lesser potential just because you think they will "fit in" to the mix. But at the same time, never forget that character matters.

Discover the "why" of the people you lead. That means you must truly come to know them by learning about their families and their experiences before they reached you.

Make sure to model and teach the value of gratefulness. When extremely talented people have joy and are truly thankful for their gifts, they become even better and more effective in their careers.

Keep everyone in the present. This is particularly important for young people with big talent and big dreams, because they have a tendency to look too far down the road. Make them understand that their aspirations will be reached by their own day-to-day demonstrated performance.

Empower your people. You must teach and support them, but

you'll only get their best when they know they are ultimately responsible for their own growth.

Understand that many of your best people will leave you, just as your own children will one day go off into the world. Create an environment in which your top people are mentors to your new people and ambassadors for your organization after they move on. The best relationships you form will be lifelong, even if you no longer work directly together.

Teach servant leadership. Each member of your team should feel that their satisfaction comes from helping those around them succeed. Organizations with servant leaders are tightly connected and driven by the deep responsibility their people feel to one another.

It's never just about the work. Your organization and the people you lead must always strive to be outward looking and do some good in the world

ACKNOWLEDGMENTS

Thank you to all the families of the players I've coached, and thank you to all the players, whether they were mentioned or not in the book. All of you are why I do what I do and you are responsible for all I've accomplished.

Michael Sokolove, who has been with me for almost three years now. Mike has attended our practices, he's gone to our meetings, met with me at my home, and spent time with me during the summer on vacations. He always picks my brain, asks me the right questions, and in the end puts it all in my voice. It's why I wanted to do this second book with him. He and I did *Players First* together in 2014 and I was so happy with how that book came out. He's one of the best and most creative writers in the business.

David Black, my literary agent, has professionally helped me in so many ways. He's been a dear friend and someone who has always had my back and encouraged me to pursue these books.

Daily I bounce things off of both Eric Lindsey and Metz Camfield, my communications team that handles our public relations, my website, and my social media. Whatever projects I'm working on, I always bring these two together and ask for their opinions and ideas, which obviously included this book. They worked actively together with me on this from the beginning to the end.

Also, DeWayne Peevy, the deputy director of athletics at Kentucky, who always puts a different set of eyes on everything that I do and whom I've come to trust immensely both professionally and as a wonderful friend.

My wife, Ellen; and my children, Erin, Megan, and Brad, who always support me and give me their insight, especially if they get a chance to correct my version of an event.

I was blessed to have three mentors, the late Jack Leaman at UMass, the late Gene Bartow, and Coach Joe B. Hall at Kentucky, who mentored me and always gave me the advice I needed to stay the course.

The athletic directors who gave me the opportunity to do what I love doing and always supported me in a way that I could be about the players. Thank you to Bob Marcum, R. C. Johnson, and Mitch Barnhart.

JOHN CALIPARI is the head coach of men's basketball at the University of Kentucky. He led the Kentucky Wildcats to the 2012 national championship and has been to a total of six Final Fours in his career, including four in a five-year period. He was inducted into the Naismith Memorial Basketball Hall of Fame in 2015. He lives in Lexington, Kentucky.